THE PRIMAL POINT

I am the Primal Point from which have been generated all created things.

The Báb

This is a period in which to recall the extraordinary heroism of the Martyr-Herald of our Faith, Whose dramatic ministry thrust humanity into a new era of history.

The months ahead will also be a time for calling to mind the lives of the Báb's intrepid followers — heroines and heroes whose faith was expressed in matchless, sacrificial acts that will forever adorn the annals of the Cause. Their qualities of fearlessness, consecration, and detachment from all save God impress themselves upon everyone who learns of their ventures. How striking, too, is the young age at which so many of those lionhearts made their indelible mark on history. During the coming period, may their example give courage to the entire company of the faithful — not least to the youth, who are once more summoned to the vanguard of a movement aimed at nothing less than the transformation of the world.

The Universal House of Justice
To the Bahá'ís of the World
Riḍván 2018

THE PRIMAL POINT

A selection of testimonials and tributes to
the Báb and His followers

Compiled by Robert Weinberg

GEORGE RONALD
OXFORD

George Ronald, Publisher
Oxford
www.grbooks.com

A catalogue record for this book is available from the British Library

ISBN 978-0-85398-619-5

Cover design: René Steiner, Steinergraphics.com

CONTENTS

INTRODUCTION

The view from the summit of Mount Carmel, overlooking the northern Israeli city of Haifa, must be one of the most arresting on the planet. The vista takes in the expansive, crescent bay of Mediterranean waters, the ancient crusader port of Akka on the opposite shore, behind which the distant white cliffs mark the border with Lebanon. Situated in the heart of the mountain, and visible from all sides, a luminous golden dome shines out as a beacon of hope in a troubled region. This majestic Shrine is encompassed by countless iridescent lights, set amidst cascading, verdant, terraced gardens, matchless in their beauty, resonant with colour, the singing of birds and the lapping of fountains. As night descends, the sloping mountainside blazes with light, from its foot to its crown. This magnificent setting provides the final resting place of Siyyid 'Alí-Muḥammad Shírazí, known to history as the Báb (1819–1850), the first of two divinely-inspired Founders of the Bahá'í Faith. At the age of 24, this pious young Merchant from Shiraz, Iran, announced His mission as a Manifestation of God.

Surrounded as His Shrine is by such conspicuous glory, it is hard to visualize that the Dispensation of the Báb began quietly with a profound conversation one May night in the year 1844, unattended by all save a single listener, a young scholar visiting the home of the Merchant. Perhaps the birth of a new religion can be likened to the undersea epi-centre of an earthquake – silent, hidden, profoundly deep, but soon afterwards destined to cause tumultuous disruption. Still, over time, the aftershocks will be noticed much further afield. The impact of that momentous announcement has since reverberated through a turbulent humanity, largely ignorant of its source, for a century and a half. Yet it is a world that is growing increasingly aware of the global Baháʾí community that has slowly taken shape following the Báb's announcement in May 1844.

For six years, between this most private of declarations and the most public of executions in 1850, the Báb revealed hundreds of thousands of verses, laying out His claims and expounding His Teachings. But it was the Báb's personal devoutness, and the cruel reception He encountered from the civil and religious authorities – along with the heroic exploits of many thousands of His followers, most of whom perished in a wave of barbaric persecution that swept through Iran – that captured the attention and the imagination of eye-witnesses, diplomats, academics and writers from the Middle East and Europe, alive to events that had such resonance with the story of Jesus Christ and His earliest supporters. The clergy and rulers of the Báb's homeland nurtured the vain hope that, with His swift demise and the brutal massacre of tens of thousands of Bábís, the religious fire He had ignited would be quenched. Yet it was their very acts that fanned the flame of fascination, resulting in the Báb's story being noised abroad further than they could have imagined.

The Báb's principal purpose was to announce the dawning of a new age for humanity and herald the coming of 'He Whom God shall make manifest', a messianic figure Who would bring an even greater message than His own.

The claim to that station was made by Bahá'u'lláh (1817–1892), born Mírzá Ḥusayn-'Alí Núrí, in Tehran. Perhaps the most socially prominent of the Báb's initial devotees, Bahá'u'lláh publicly announced in 1863 that He was the One promised by the Báb, as well as the fulfilment of the expectations of the Abrahamic and other major religions. In more than a hundred volumes of Writings, Bahá'u'lláh delivered a vast new Revelation of guidance from God to humanity, outlining a framework for the development of a global civilization which would take into account all of the manifold spiritual and material dimensions of human life.

❧

'The towering grandeur and the tender beauty of the life of a Manifestation of God cannot be comprehended by events usually associated with a saintly life,' wrote the distinguished scholar of the Bahá'í Faith, Hasan M. Balyuzi.

The immensity of such a life presents itself in that mysterious influence which it exerts over countless lives, an influence which functions not through social status and prestige, wealth, secular power or worldly dominion; indeed not even through a medium of mere superior knowledge and intellectual achievement.

The Manifestation of God is the Archetype, and His life is the supreme pattern. His vision, not arrested by time and space, encompasses the future as well as the past. He is the only and the necessary link between one period of social evolution and another. Without Him history is meaningless and coordination is impossible. Furthermore, the Manifestation of God releases deep reservoirs of spiritual power and quickens the forces

latent in humanity. By Him, and by Him alone, can
Man attain 'second birth'.[1]

While the tender beauty of the life of the Báb and the valour
of the Bábís have been recounted in numerous texts – not
least in Nabíl-i-Zarandí's superlative narrative of the early
history of the Bahá'í Faith and in Balyuzí's seminal biog-
raphy – the purpose of this present anthology, collected to
mark the bicentenary of the Báb's birth, is to collect together
some of the many tributes and testimonials to the Báb
that capture, not so much the chronological details of His
earthly life, but rather the importance of His station, the
impact of His Revelation and the commotion it generated.

Foremost among these are those tributes penned by
Bahá'u'lláh Himself. In many of His Writings, He pays
touching homage to His Martyr-Herald and to the sacrifices made by the Báb, and those who believed in Him,
to usher in a new day for humanity. Bahá'u'lláh's son and
successor 'Abdu'l-Bahá (1844–1921) further conveyed
the implications of the Báb's advent, during His historic
journeys west to nurture fledgling Bahá'í communities in
Europe and North America.

In turn, Shoghi Effendi (1897–1957), 'Abdu'l-Bahá's
grandson and the Guardian of the Bahá'í Faith after His
passing, elucidated in his own peerless prose – for those
members of a movement that was becoming increasingly
global throughout the twentieth century – the exact nature
of the Báb's station, not only as the forerunner to the Promised One of all ages, but as a Manifestation of God in His
own right:

We behold, as we survey the episodes of this first act
of a sublime drama, the figure of its Master Hero, the

Báb, arise meteor-like above the horizon of S͟híráz, traverse the sombre sky of Persia from south to north, decline with tragic swiftness, and perish in a blaze of glory. We see His satellites, a galaxy of God-intoxicated heroes, mount above that same horizon, irradiate that same incandescent light, burn themselves out with that self-same swiftness, and impart in their turn an added impetus to the steadily gathering momentum of God's nascent Faith.[2]

❧

The mission undertaken by the Báb, and the daring, fearless acts of His followers have much resonance today, perhaps more so than ever before. As the Universal House of Justice – the elected, international governing council of the Bahá'í community – has pointed out:

> Though separated from our own time by two centuries, the society in which the Báb appeared resembles the present-day world for the sense of oppression and for the longing of so many to find answers to slake the soul's thirst to know.[3]

Foremost among those in possession of such a thirst are the young. Writing on 1 July 2013 to the attendees of 114 Bahá'í youth conferences around the world, the Universal House of Justice observed:

> When the exalted figure of the Báb, aged just twenty-five, arose to deliver His revolutionizing message to the world, many among those who accepted and spread His teachings were young, even younger than the Báb

Himself. Their heroism, immortalized in all its dazzling intensity in *The Dawn-Breakers*, will illumine the annals of human history for centuries to come. Thus began a pattern in which every generation of youth, drawing inspiration from the same divine impulse to cast the world anew, has seized the opportunity to contribute to the latest stage in the unfolding process that is to transform the life of humankind. It is a pattern that has suffered no interruption from the time of the Báb to this present hour.[4]

It is hoped that this anthology will be of particular inspiration to the Baháʼí youth, who follow so conscientiously and with such ardour in the footsteps of their God-intoxicated, spiritual forebears.

ๆ

In 2009, exactly one hundred years after the interment of the remains of the Báb on Mount Carmel, the Universal House of Justice observed that, 'The sacrifices of the Báb and the dawn-breakers of the Cause are yielding abundant fruit. . . . The magnificent progress achieved over the past century demonstrates the invincible power with which the Cause is endowed.'[5]

Now, each year, Baháʼí pilgrims from every spot on the planet arrive to circumambulate the Báb's sacred Shrine before entering to pray and meditate. His vision, first delineated in the middle of the nineteenth century – of humanity in all its variegated diversity, moving towards the Cause of 'Him Whom God shall make manifest', as one soul in many bodies – has become a reality, one which demonstrates the futility of any attempts to snuff out this inextinguishable light. 'It is but a portent of the ultimate realization of the oneness of humankind.'[6]

'That is why the Bábí teachings,' stated the great Russian writer Leo Tolstoy, '. . . insofar as they hold fast to their main and fundamental ideas of brotherhood, equality and love, are assured a great future.'[7]

Robert Weinberg
London, 2019

I

FROM THE WRITINGS OF
BAHÁ'U'LLÁH

From the Writings of Bahá'u'lláh

We, verily, believe in Him Who, in the person of the Báb, hath been sent down by the Will of the one true God, the King of Kings, the All-Praised.[8]

❧

Upon His brow there shone a beauteous crown, which cast its splendour upon all who are in heaven and all who are on earth. Rejoice! This is the immortal Youth, come with a mighty cause.[9]

❧

Contemplate with thine inward eye the chain of successive Revelations that hath linked the Manifestation of Adam with that of the Báb. I testify before God that each one of these Manifestations hath been sent down through the operation of the Divine Will and Purpose, that each hath been the bearer of a specific Message, that each hath been entrusted with a divinely revealed Book and been commissioned to unravel the mysteries of a mighty Tablet. The measure of the Revelation with which every one of them hath been identified had been definitely foreordained. This, verily, is a token of Our favour unto them, if ye be of those that comprehend this truth.[10]

❧

O Aḥmad! Bear thou witness that verily He is God and there is no God but Him, the King, the Protector, the Incomparable, the Omnipotent. And that the One Whom He hath sent forth by the name of 'Alí [The Báb] was the true One from God, to Whose commands we are all conforming.

Say: O people be obedient to the ordinances of God, which have been enjoined in the Bayán by the Glorious, the Wise One. Verily He is the King of the Messengers and His Book is the Mother Book did ye but know.[11]

✺

Magnify Thou, O Lord my God, Him Who is the Primal Point, the Divine Mystery, the Unseen Essence, the Dayspring of Divinity, and the Manifestation of Thy Lordship, through Whom all the knowledge of the past and all the knowledge of the future were made plain, through Whom the pearls of Thy hidden wisdom were uncovered, and the mystery of Thy treasured name disclosed, Whom Thou hast appointed as the Announcer of the One through Whose name the letter B and the letter E have been joined and united, through Whom Thy majesty, Thy sovereignty and Thy might were made known, through Whom Thy words have been sent down, and Thy laws set forth with clearness, and Thy signs spread abroad, and Thy Word established, through Whom the hearts of Thy chosen ones were laid bare, and all that were in the heavens and all that were on the earth were gathered together, Whom Thou hast called 'Alí-Muḥammad in the kingdom of Thy names, and the Spirit of Spirits in the Tablets of Thine irrevocable decree, Whom Thou hast invested with Thine own title, unto Whose name all other names have, at Thy bidding and through the power of Thy might, been made to return, and in Whom Thou hast caused all Thine attributes and titles to attain their final consummation. To Him also belong such names as lay hid within Thy stainless tabernacles, in Thine invisible world and Thy sanctified cities.[12]

❧

. . . all names and attributes revolve round His Essence and circle about the threshold of His sanctuary. For He it is Who traineth all names, revealeth all attributes, conferreth life upon all beings, proclaimeth the divine verses, and arrayeth the heavenly signs. Nay, shouldst thou gaze with thine inner eye, thou wouldst find that all save Him fade into utter nothingness and are as a thing forgotten in His holy presence.[13]

❧

Ages rolled away, until they attained their consummation in this, the Lord of days, the Day whereon the Daystar of the Bayán manifested itself above the horizon of mercy, the Day in which the Beauty of the All-Glorious shone forth in the exalted person of 'Alí-Muḥammad, the Báb. No sooner did He reveal Himself, than all the people rose up against Him. By some He was denounced as one that hath uttered slanders against God, the Almighty, the Ancient of Days. Others regarded Him as a man smitten with madness, an allegation which I, Myself, have heard from the lips of one of the divines. Still others disputed His claim to be the Mouthpiece of God, and stigmatized Him as one who had stolen and used as his the words of the Almighty, who had perverted their meaning, and mingled them with his own. The Eye of Grandeur weepeth sore for the things which their mouths have uttered, while they continue to rejoice upon their seats.

'God,' said He, 'is My witness, O people! I am come to you with a Revelation from the Lord, your God, the Lord of your fathers of old. Look not, O people, at the things ye possess. Look rather at the things God hath sent down unto you. This, surely, will be better for you than the whole of creation, could ye but perceive it. Repeat the gaze, O people, and consider the testimony of God and His proof which are in your possession, and compare them unto the Revelation sent down unto you in this Day, that the truth, the infallible truth, may be indubitably manifested unto you. Follow not, O people, the steps of the Evil One; follow ye the Faith of the All-Merciful, and be ye of them that truly believe. What would it profit man, if he were to fail to recognize the Revelation of God? Nothing whatever. To this Mine own Self, the Omnipotent, the Omniscient, the All-Wise, will testify.'

The more He exhorted them, the fiercer grew their enmity, till, at the last, they put Him to death with shameful cruelty. The curse of God be upon the oppressors!

A few believed in Him; few of Our servants are the thankful. These He admonished, in all His Tablets – nay, in every passage of His wondrous writings – not to give themselves up in the Day of the promised Revelation to anything whatever, be it in the heaven or in the earth. 'O people!' said He, 'I have revealed Myself for His Manifestation, and have caused My Book, the Bayán, to descend upon you for no other purpose except to establish the truth of His Cause. Fear ye God, and contend not with Him as the people of the Qur'án have contended with Me. At whatever time ye hear of Him, hasten ye towards Him, and cleave ye to whatsoever He may reveal unto you. Naught else besides Him can ever profit you, no, not though ye produce from first to last the testimonies of all those who were before you.'

And when after the lapse of a few years the heaven of Divine decree was cleft asunder, and the Beauty of the Báb appeared in the clouds of the names of God, arrayed in a new raiment, these same people maliciously rose up against

Him, Whose light embraceth all created things. They broke
His Covenant, rejected His truth, contended with Him,
caviled at His signs, treated His testimony as falsehood, and
joined the company of the infidels. Eventually, they determined to take away His life. Such is the state of them who
are in a far-gone error![14]

❧

Though young and tender of age, and though the Cause He
revealed was contrary to the desire of all the peoples of the
earth, both high and low, rich and poor, exalted and abased,
king and subject, yet He arose and steadfastly proclaimed
it. All have known and heard this. He was afraid of no one;
He was regardless of consequences. Could such a thing be
made manifest except through the power of a divine Revelation, and the potency of God's invincible Will? By the
righteousness of God! Were any one to entertain so great a
Revelation in his heart, the thought of such a declaration
would alone confound him! Were the hearts of all men to
be crowded into his heart, he would still hesitate to venture
upon so awful an enterprise. He could achieve it only by
the permission of God, only if the channel of his heart were
to be linked with the Source of divine grace, and his soul
be assured of the unfailing sustenance of the Almighty. To
what, We wonder, do they ascribe so great a daring? Do
they accuse Him of folly as they accused the Prophets of
old? Or do they maintain that His motive was none other
than leadership and the acquisition of earthly riches?

Gracious God! In His Book, which He hath entitled
'Qayyúmu'l-Asmá', – the first, the greatest, and mightiest
of all books – He prophesied His own martyrdom. In it is
this passage: 'O Thou Remnant of God! I have sacrificed

myself wholly for Thee; I have accepted curses for Thy sake; and have yearned for naught but martyrdom in the path of Thy love. Sufficient Witness unto me is God, the Exalted, the Protector, the Ancient of Days!'

. . . Could the Revealer of such utterance be regarded as walking in any other way than the way of God, and as having yearned for aught else except His good-pleasure? In this very verse there lieth concealed a breath of detachment, which if it were breathed full upon the world, all beings would renounce their life, and sacrifice their souls.

. . . And now consider how this Sadrih of the Riḍván of God hath, in the prime of youth, risen to proclaim the Cause of God. Behold what steadfastness that Beauty of God hath revealed. The whole world rose to hinder Him, yet it utterly failed. The more severe the persecution they inflicted on that Sadrih of Blessedness, the more His fervour increased, and the brighter burned the flame of His love. All this is evident, and none disputeth its truth. Finally, He surrendered His soul, and winged His flight unto the realms above.

. . . No sooner had that eternal Beauty revealed Himself in S̲h̲íráz, in the year sixty, and rent asunder the veil of concealment, than the signs of the ascendancy, the might, the sovereignty, and power, emanating from that Essence of Essences and Sea of Seas, were manifest in every land. So much so, that from every city there appeared the signs, the evidences, the tokens, the testimonies of that Divine Luminary. How many were those pure and kindly hearts which faithfully reflected the light of that eternal Sun, and how manifold the emanations of knowledge from that Ocean of divine wisdom which encompassed all beings! In every city, all the divines and dignatories rose to hinder and repress them, and girded up the loins of malice, of envy, and tyranny for their suppression. How great the number of those holy souls, those essences of justice, who, accused of tyranny, were put to death! And how many embodiments of purity, who showed forth naught but true knowledge and stainless deeds, suffered an agonising death! Notwithstanding all this, each of these holy beings, up to his last moment, breathed the Name of God, and soared in the realm of submission and resignation. Such was the potency and transmuting influence which He exercised over them, that they ceased to cherish any desire but His will, and wedded their souls to His remembrance.

Reflect: Who in the world is able to manifest such transcendent power, such pervading influence? All these stainless hearts and sanctified souls have, with absolute resignation, responded to the summons of His decree. Instead of complaining, they rendered thanks unto God, and, amidst the darkness of their anguish they revealed naught but radiant acquiescence to His will. It is evident how relentless was the hate, and how bitter the malice and enmity entertained by all the peoples of the earth towards these companions. The persecution and pain they inflicted on these holy and spiritual beings were regarded by them as means unto salvation, prosperity, and everlasting success. Hath the world, since the days of Adam, witnessed such tumult, such violent commotion? Notwithstanding all the torture they suffered, and the manifold afflictions they endured, they became the object of universal opprobrium and execration. Methinks, patience was revealed only by virtue of their fortitude, and faithfulness itself was begotten only by their deeds.

Do thou ponder these momentous happenings in thy heart, so that thou mayest apprehend the greatness of this Revelation, and perceive its stupendous glory.[15]

☙

Had the Primal Point been someone else beside Me as ye claim, and had attained My presence, verily He would have never allowed Himself to be separated from Me, but rather We would have had mutual delights with each other in My Days. He, in truth, wept sore in His remoteness from Me. He preceded Me that He might summon the people unto My Kingdom, as it hath been set forth in the Tablets, could ye but perceive it![16]

❧

Wherefore thou hast been singled out by God through the tongue of thy Lord, the Báb, the brightness of Whose countenance hath enveloped, and will continue to envelop, the whole of creation. Render thanks unto the Almighty, and magnify His name, inasmuch as He hath aided thee to recognize a Cause that hath made the hearts of the inhabitants of the heavens and of the earth to tremble, that hath caused the denizens of the Kingdoms of creation and of Revelation to cry out, and through which the hidden secrets of men's breasts have been searched out and tested.[17]

❧

Do Thou bless, O Lord my God, the Primal Point, through Whom the point of creation hath been made to revolve in both the visible and invisible worlds, Whom Thou hast designated as the One whereunto should return whatsoever must return unto Thee, and as the Revealer of whatsoever may be manifested by Thee. Do Thou also bless such of His Letters as have not turned away from Thee, who have been firmly established in Thy love, and clung steadfastly to Thy good-pleasure. Bless Thou, likewise, as long as Thine own

Self endureth and Thine own Essence doth last, them that have suffered martyrdom in Thy path. Thou art, verily, the Ever-Forgiving, the Most Merciful.[18]

ৎ১

The more He extolled the remembrance of God, the greater they waxed in their oppression, until all the divines pronounced sentence against Him, save those that were acquainted with the precepts of God, the All-Glorious, the Best-Beloved. Matters came to such a pass that they united to put Him to death. They suspended Him in the air, and the hosts of misbelief flung at Him the bullets of malice and hatred, piercing the body of the One unto Whom the Holy Spirit is a humble servant, the dust of Whose feet is the object of adoration of the Concourse on high, and from Whose very sandals the inmates of Paradise seek a blessing. Whereupon the inhabitants of the unseen realm wept sore beneath the pavilion of eternity, the pillars of the Throne trembled, the inmost realities of all things were stirred into commotion, and the divine Tree received its full measure of His gleaming blood which was shed upon the earth.

Erelong will God reveal the mystery of this Tree, make it to flourish through the power of truth, and cause it to intone: 'Verily I am God, there is none other God but Him. All are My servants whom We have created to carry out My bidding, and by My bidding they all, verily, abide.'[19]

2

FROM THE WRITINGS AND
TALKS OF 'ABDU'L-BAHÁ

From the Writings and Talks of 'Abdu'l-Bahá

He was entitled the Báb, which means *door* or *gate*. The bearer of this title was a great Soul from Whom spiritual signs and evidences became manifest. He withstood the tests of time and lived contrary to the custom and usages of Persia. He revealed a new system of faith opposed to the beliefs in His country and promulgated certain principles contrary to the thoughts of the people. For this, that remarkable Personality was imprisoned by the Persian government. Eventually, by order of the government He was martyred. The account of this martyrdom, briefly stated, is as follows: He was suspended in a square as a target and shot to death. This revered Personage foreshadowed the advent of another Soul of Whom He said, 'When He cometh He shall reveal greater things unto you.'[20]

❦

As for the Báb – may my soul be His sacrifice! – it was at a young age, that is, in the twenty-fifth year of His blessed life, that He arose to proclaim His Cause. Among the Shí'ihs it is universally acknowledged that He never studied in any school, nor acquired learning from any teacher. To this the people of Shíráz, each and all, bear witness. Nevertheless, He suddenly appeared before the people, endowed with consummate knowledge, and though but a merchant, confounded all the divines of Persia. Alone, He undertook a task that can scarcely be conceived, for the Persians are known throughout the world for their religious fanaticism. This illustrious Being arose with such power as to shake the foundations of the religious laws, customs, manners, morals, and habits of Persia, and instituted a new law, faith,

23

and religion. Though the eminent men of the State, the majority of the people, and the leaders of religion arose one and all to destroy and annihilate Him, He single-handedly withstood them and set all of Persia in motion. How numerous the divines, the leaders, and the inhabitants of that land who with perfect joy and gladness offered up their lives in His path and hastened to the field of martyrdom!

The government, the nation, the clergy, and prominent leaders sought to extinguish His light, but to no avail. At last His moon rose, His star shone forth, His foundation was secured, and His horizon was flooded with light. He trained a large multitude through divine education and exerted a marvellous influence upon the thoughts, customs, morals, and manners of the Persians. He proclaimed the glad-tidings of the manifestation of the Sun of Bahá to all His followers and readied them for faith and certitude.

The manifestation of such marvellous signs and mighty undertakings, the influence exerted upon the thoughts and minds of the people, the laying of the foundations of progress, and the establishment of the prerequisites of success and prosperity by a young merchant constitute the greatest proof that He was a universal Educator – a fact that no fair-minded person would ever hesitate to acknowledge.[21]

༄

This is 23 May, the anniversary of the message and Declaration of the Báb. It is a blessed day and the dawn of manifestation, for the appearance of the Báb was the early light of the true morn, whereas the manifestation of the Blessed Beauty, Bahá'u'lláh, was the shining forth of the sun. Therefore, it is a blessed day, the inception of the heavenly bounty, the beginning of the divine effulgence. On this day in 1844 the Báb was sent forth heralding and proclaiming the Kingdom of God, announcing the glad tidings of the coming of Bahá'u'lláh and withstanding the opposition of the whole Persian nation. Some of the Persians followed Him. For this they suffered the most grievous difficulties and severe ordeals. They withstood the tests with wonderful power and sublime heroism. Thousands were cast into prison, punished, persecuted and martyred. Their homes were pillaged and destroyed, their possessions confiscated. They sacrificed their lives most willingly and remained unshaken in their faith to the very end. Those wonderful souls are the lamps of God, the stars of sanctity shining gloriously from the eternal horizon of the will of God.

The Báb was subjected to bitter persecution in Shíráz, where He first proclaimed His mission and message. A period of famine afflicted that region, and the Báb journeyed to Iṣfahán. There the learned men rose against Him in great hostility. He was arrested and sent to Tabríz. From thence He was transferred to Mákú and finally imprisoned in the strong castle of Chihríq. Afterward He was martyred in Tabríz.

This is merely an outline of the history of the Báb. He withstood all persecutions and bore every suffering and ordeal with unflinching strength. The more His enemies endeavoured to extinguish that flame, the brighter it became. Day by day His Cause spread and strengthened. During the time when He was among the people He was constantly heralding the coming of Bahá'u'lláh. In all His Books and Tablets He mentioned Bahá'u'lláh and announced the glad tidings of His manifestation, prophesying that He would reveal Himself in the ninth year. He said that in the ninth year 'you will attain to all happiness'; in the ninth year 'you will be blessed with the meeting of the Promised One of Whom I have spoken'. He mentioned the Blessed Perfection, Bahá'u'lláh, by the title

'Him Whom God shall make manifest'. In brief, that blessed
Soul offered His very life in the pathway of Bahá'u'lláh, even
as it is recorded in historical writings and records. In His first
Book, the Best of Stories, He says, 'O Remnant of God! I am
wholly sacrificed to Thee; I am content with curses in Thy
path; I crave nought but to be slain in Thy love; and God, the
Supreme, sufficeth as an eternal protection.'

Consider how the Báb endured difficulties and tribula-
tions; how He gave His life in the Cause of God; how He
was attracted to the love of the Blessed Beauty, Bahá'u'lláh;
and how He announced the glad tidings of His manifestation. We must follow His heavenly example; we must be
self-sacrificing and aglow with the fire of the love of God.
We must partake of the bounty and grace of the Lord, for
the Báb has admonished us to arise in service to the Cause
of God, to be absolutely severed from all else save God
during the day of the Blessed Perfection, Bahá'u'lláh, to be
completely attracted by the love of Bahá'u'lláh, to love all
humanity for His sake, to be lenient and merciful to all for
Him and to upbuild the oneness of the world of humanity.[22]

✑

As soon as the Báb revealed His Cause, Bahá'u'lláh proclaimed: 'This great Man is the Lord of the righteous, and it
is incumbent upon all to bear allegiance unto Him.'[23]

✑

If the Báb had not manifested love for mankind, surely he
would not have offered his breast for a thousand bullets.[24]

✑

Why did the Báb make the supreme sacrifice and why did Bahá'u'lláh pass the years of His life in prison?

Why should all this suffering have been, if not to prove the everlasting life of the spirit?[25]

3

FROM THE WRITINGS OF
SHOGHI EFFENDI

From the Writings of Shoghi Effendi

May 23, 1844, signalizes the commencement of the most turbulent period of the Heroic Age of the Bahá'í Era, an age which marks the opening of the most glorious epoch in the greatest cycle which the spiritual history of mankind has yet witnessed. No more than a span of nine short years marks the duration of this most spectacular, this most tragic, this most eventful period of the first Bahá'í century. It was ushered in by the birth of a Revelation whose Bearer posterity will acclaim as the '*Point round Whom the realities of the Prophets and Messengers revolve*,' and terminated with the first stirrings of a still more potent Revelation, '*whose day*,' Bahá'u'lláh Himself affirms, '*every Prophet hath announced*,' for which '*the soul of every Divine Messenger hath thirsted*,' and through which '*God hath proved the hearts of the entire company of His Messengers and Prophets*.' Little wonder that the immortal chronicler of the events associated with the birth and rise of the Bahá'í Revelation has seen fit to devote no less than half of his moving narrative to the description of those happenings that have during such a brief space of time so greatly enriched, through their tragedy and heroism, the religious annals of mankind. In sheer dramatic power, in the rapidity with which events of momentous importance succeeded each other, in the holocaust which baptized its birth, in the miraculous circumstances attending the martyrdom of the One Who had ushered it in, in the potentialities with which it had been from the outset so thoroughly impregnated, in the forces to which it eventually gave birth, this nine-year period may well rank as unique in the whole range of man's religious experience. We behold, as we survey the episodes of this first act of a sublime drama, the figure of its Master Hero, the Báb, arise meteor-like above the horizon of Shíráz, traverse the sombre sky of Persia from south to north, decline with tragic swiftness, and perish in a blaze of glory. We see His satellites, a galaxy of God-intoxicated heroes, mount above that same horizon, irradiate that same incandescent light, burn themselves out with that self-same swiftness, and impart in their turn an added impetus to the steadily gathering momentum of God's nascent Faith.

He Who communicated the original impulse to so incalculable a Movement was none other than the promised Qá'im (He who ariseth), the Ṣáḥibu'z-Zamán (the Lord of the Age), Who assumed the exclusive right of annulling the whole Qur'ánic Dispensation, Who styled Himself '*the Primal Point from which have been generated all created things . . . the Countenance of God Whose splendor can never be obscured, the Light of God Whose radiance can never fade.*' The people among whom He appeared were the most decadent race in the civilized world, grossly ignorant, savage, cruel, steeped in prejudice, servile in their submission to an almost deified hierarchy, recalling in their abjectness the Israelites of Egypt in the days of Moses, in their fanaticism the Jews in the days of Jesus, and in their perversity the idolators of Arabia in the days of Muḥammad. The arch-enemy who repudiated His claim, challenged His authority, persecuted His Cause, succeeded in almost quenching His light, and who eventually became disintegrated under the impact of His Revelation was the Shí'ah priesthood. Fiercely fanatic, unspeakably corrupt, enjoying unlimited ascendancy over the masses, jealous of their position, and irreconcilably opposed to all liberal ideas, the members of this caste had for one thousand years invoked the name of the Hidden Imám, their breasts had glowed with the expectation of His advent, their pulpits had rung with the praises of His world-embracing dominion, their lips were still devoutly and perpetually murmuring prayers for the hastening of His coming. The willing tools who prostituted their high office for the accomplishment of the enemy's designs were no less than the sovereigns of the Qájár dynasty, first, the bigoted, the sickly, the vacillating Muḥammad Sháh, who at the last moment cancelled the Báb's imminent visit to the capital, and, second, the youthful and inexperienced Náṣiri'd-Dín Sháh, who gave his ready assent to the sentence of his Captive's death. The arch villains who joined hands with the prime movers of so wicked a conspiracy were the two grand vizirs, Ḥájí Mírzá Áqásí, the idolized tutor of Muḥammad Sháh, a vulgar, false-hearted and fickle-minded schemer, and the arbitrary, bloodthirsty, reckless Amír-Niẓám, Mírzá Taqí Khán, the first of whom exiled the Báb to the mountain fastnesses of Ádhirbáyján, and the latter decreed His death in Tabríz. Their accomplice in these and other heinous crimes was a government bolstered up by a flock of idle, parasitical princelings and governors, corrupt, incompetent, tenaciously holding to their ill-gotten privileges, and utterly subservient to a notoriously degraded clerical order. The heroes whose deeds shine upon the record of this fierce spiritual contest, involving at once people, clergy, monarch and government, were the Báb's chosen disciples, the Letters of the Living, and their companions, the trail-breakers of the New Day, who to so much intrigue, ignorance, depravity, cruelty, superstition and cowardice opposed a spirit exalted, unquenchable and awe-inspiring, a knowledge surprisingly profound, an eloquence sweeping in its force, a piety unexcelled in fervor, a courage leonine in its fierceness, a self-abnegation saintly in its purity, a resolve granite-like in its firmness, a vision stupendous in its range, a veneration for the Prophet and His Imáms disconcerting to their adversaries, a power of persuasion alarming to their antagonists, a standard of faith and a code of conduct that challenged and revolutionized the lives of their countrymen.[26]

༄

Thus ended a life which posterity will recognize as standing at the confluence of two universal prophetic cycles, the Adamic Cycle stretching back as far as the first dawnings of the world's recorded religious history and the Bahá'í Cycle destined to propel itself across the unborn reaches of time for a period of no less than five thousand centuries. The apotheosis in which such a life attained its consummation marks, as already observed, the culmination of the most heroic phase of the Heroic Age of the Bahá'í Dispensation. It can, moreover, be regarded in no other light except as the most dramatic, the most tragic event transpiring within the entire range of the first Bahá'í century. Indeed it can be rightly acclaimed as unparalleled in the annals of the lives of all the Founders of the world's existing religious systems. . . .

It would indeed be no exaggeration to say that nowhere in the whole compass of the world's religious literature, except in the Gospels, do we find any record relating to the death of any of the religion-founders of the past comparable to the martyrdom suffered by the Prophet of Shíráz. So strange, so inexplicable a phenomenon, attested by eyewitnesses, corroborated by men of recognized standing, and acknowledged by government as well as unofficial historians among the people who had sworn undying hostility to the Bábí Faith, may be truly regarded as the most marvelous manifestation of the unique potentialities with which a Dispensation promised by all the Dispensations of the past had been endowed. The passion of Jesus Christ, and indeed

34

His whole public ministry, alone offer a parallel to the Mission and death of the Báb, a parallel which no student of comparative religion can fail to perceive or ignore. In the youthfulness and meekness of the Inaugurator of the Bábí Dispensation; in the extreme brevity and turbulence of His public ministry; in the dramatic swiftness with which that ministry moved towards its climax; in the apostolic order which He instituted, and the primacy which He conferred on one of its members; in the boldness of His challenge to the time-honored conventions, rites and laws which had been woven into the fabric of the religion He Himself had been born into; in the rôle which an officially recognized and firmly entrenched religious hierarchy played as chief instigator of the outrages which He was made to suffer; in the indignities heaped upon Him; in the suddenness of His arrest; in the interrogation to which He was subjected; in the derision poured, and the scourging inflicted, upon Him; in the public affront He sustained; and, finally, in His ignominious suspension before the gaze of a hostile multitude – in all these we cannot fail to discern a remarkable similarity to the distinguishing features of the career of Jesus Christ.

It should be remembered, however, that apart from the miracle associated with the Báb's execution, He, unlike the Founder of the Christian religion, is not only to be regarded as the independent Author of a divinely revealed Dispensation, but must also be recognized as the Herald of a new Era and the Inaugurator of a great universal prophetic cycle. Nor should the important fact be overlooked that, whereas the chief adversaries of Jesus Christ, in His lifetime, were the Jewish rabbis and their associates, the forces arrayed against the Báb represented the combined civil and ecclesiastical powers of Persia, which, from the moment of His declaration to the hour of His death, persisted, unitedly and by every means at their disposal, in conspiring against the upholders and in vilifying the tenets of His Revelation.

The Báb, acclaimed by Bahá'u'lláh as the '*Essence of Essences*,' the '*Sea of Seas*,' the '*Point round Whom the realities of the Prophets and Messengers revolve*,' '*from Whom God hath caused to proceed the knowledge of all that was and shall be*,' Whose '*rank excelleth that of all the Prophets*,' and Whose '*Revelation transcendeth the comprehension and understanding of all their chosen ones*,' had delivered His Message and discharged His mission. He Who was, in the words of 'Abdu'l-Bahá, the '*Morn of Truth*' and '*Harbinger of the Most Great Light*,' Whose advent at once signalized the termination of the '*Prophetic Cycle*' and the inception of the '*Cycle of Fulfillment*,' had simultaneously through His Revelation banished the shades of night that had descended upon His country, and proclaimed the impending rise of that Incomparable Orb Whose radiance was to envelop the whole of mankind. He, as affirmed by Himself, '*the Primal Point from which have been generated all created things*,' '*one of the sustaining pillars of the Primal Word of God*,' the '*Mystic Fane*,' the '*Great Announcement*,' the '*Flame of that supernal Light that glowed upon Sinai*,' the '*Remembrance of God*' concerning Whom '*a separate Covenant hath been established with each and every Prophet*' had, through His advent, at once fulfilled the promise of all ages and ushered in the consummation of all Revelations. He the 'Qá'im' (He Who ariseth) promised to the Shí'ahs, the 'Mihdí' (One Who is guided) awaited by the Sunnís, the 'Return of John the Baptist' expected by the Christians, the 'Úshídar-Máh' referred to in the Zoroastrian scriptures, the 'Return of Elijah' anticipated by the Jews, Whose Revelation was to show forth '*the signs and tokens of all the Prophets*', Who was to '*manifest the perfection of Moses, the radiance of Jesus and the patience of Job*' had appeared, proclaimed His Cause, been mercilessly persecuted and died gloriously. The *'Second Woe,'* spoken of in the Apocalypse of St. John the Divine, had, at long last, appeared, and the first of the two *'Messengers,'* Whose appearance had been prophesied in the Qur'án, had been sent down. The first *'Trumpet-Blast,'* destined to smite the earth with extermination, announced in the latter Book, had finally been sounded. *'The Inevitable,' 'The Catastrophe,' 'The Resurrection,' 'The Earthquake of the Last Hour,'* foretold by that same Book, had all come to pass. The *'clear tokens'* had been *'sent down,'* and the *'Spirit'* had *'breathed,'* and the *'souls'* had *'waked up,'* and the *'heaven'* had been *'cleft,'* and the *'angels'* had *'ranged in order,'* and the *'stars'* had been *'blotted out,'* and the *'earth'* had *'cast forth her burden,'* and *'Paradise'* had been *'brought near,'* and *'hell'* had been *'made to blaze,'* and the *'Book'* had been *'set,'* and the *'Bridge'* had been *'laid out,'* and the *'Balance'* had been *'set up,'* and the *'mountains scattered in dust.'* The *'cleansing of the Sanctuary,'* prophesied by Daniel and confirmed by Jesus Christ in His reference to *'the abomination of desolation,'* had been accomplished. The *'day whose length shall be a thousand years,'* foretold by the Apostle of God in His Book, had terminated. The *'forty and two months,'* during which the *'Holy City,'* as predicted by St. John the Divine, would be trodden under foot, had elapsed. The *'time of the end'* had been ushered in, and the first of the *'two Witnesses'* into Whom, *'after three days and a half the Spirit of Life from God'* would enter, had arisen and had *'ascended up to heaven in a cloud.'* The *'remaining twenty and five letters to be made manifest,'* according to Islamic tradition, out of the *'twenty and seven letters'* of which Knowledge has been declared to consist, had been revealed. The *'Man Child,'* mentioned in the Book of Revelation, destined to '*rule all nations with a rod of iron,*' had released, through His coming, the creative energies which, reinforced by the effusions of a swiftly succeeding and infinitely mightier Revelation, were to instill into the entire human race the capacity to achieve its organic unification, attain maturity and thereby reach the final stage in its age-long evolution. The clarion-call addressed to the '*concourse of kings and of the sons of kings,*' marking the inception of a process which, accelerated by Bahá'u'lláh's subsequent warnings to the entire company of the monarchs of East and West, was to produce so widespread a revolution in the fortunes of royalty, had been raised in the Qayyúmú'l-Asmá'. The '*Order,*' whose foundation the Promised One was to establish in the Kitáb-i-Aqdas, and the features of which the Center of the Covenant was to delineate in His Testament, and whose administrative framework the entire body of His followers are now erecting, had been categorically announced in the Persian Bayán. The laws which were designed, on the one hand, to abolish at a stroke the privileges and ceremonials, the ordinances and institutions of a superannuated Dispensation, and to bridge, on the other, the gap between an obsolete system and the institutions of a world-encompassing Order destined to supersede it, had been clearly formulated and proclaimed. The Covenant which, despite the determined assaults launched against it, succeeded, unlike all previous Dispensations, in preserving the integrity of the Faith of its Author, and in paving the way for the advent of the One Who was to be its Center and Object, had been firmly and irrevocably established. The light which, throughout successive periods, was to propagate itself gradually from its cradle as far as Vancouver in the West and the China Sea in the East, and to diffuse its radiance as far as Iceland in the

North and the Tasman Sea in the South, had broken. The forces of darkness, at first confined to the concerted hostility of the civil and ecclesiastical powers of Shí'ah Persia, gathering momentum, at a later stage, through the avowed and persistent opposition of the Caliph of Islám and the Sunní hierarchy in Turkey, and destined to culminate in the fierce antagonism of the sacerdotal orders associated with other and still more powerful religious systems, had launched their initial assault. The nucleus of the divinely ordained, world-embracing Community – a Community whose infant strength had already plucked asunder the fetters of Shí'ah orthodoxy, and which was, with every expansion in the range of its fellowship, to seek and obtain a wider and still more significant recognition of its claims to be the world religion of the future, had been formed and was slowly crystallizing. And, lastly, the seed, endowed by the Hand of Omnipotence with such vast potentialities, though rudely trampled under foot and seemingly perished from the face of the earth, had, through this very process, been vouchsafed the opportunity to germinate and remanifest itself, in the shape of a still more compelling Revelation – a Revelation destined to blossom forth, in a later period into the flourishing institutions of a world-wide administrative System, and to ripen, in the Golden Age as yet unborn, into mighty agencies functioning in consonance with the principles of a world-unifying, world-redeeming Order.[27]

ഇ

Dearly-beloved friends! That the Báb, the inaugurator of the Bábí Dispensation, is fully entitled to rank as one of the self-sufficient Manifestations of God, that He has been invested with sovereign power and authority, and exercises all the rights and prerogatives of independent Prophethood, is yet another fundamental verity which the Message of Bahá'u'lláh insistently proclaims and which its followers must uncompromisingly uphold. That He is not to be regarded merely as an inspired Precursor of the Bahá'í Revelation, that in His person, as He Himself bears witness in the Persian Bayán, the object of all the Prophets gone before Him has been fulfilled, is a truth which I feel it my duty to demonstrate and emphasize. We would assuredly be failing in our duty to the Faith we profess and would be violating one of its basic and sacred principles if in our words or by our conduct we hesitate to recognize the implications of this root principle of Bahá'í belief, or refuse to uphold unreservedly its integrity and demonstrate its truth. Indeed the chief motive actuating me to undertake the task of editing and translating Nabíl's immortal Narrative has been to enable every follower of the Faith in the West to better understand and more readily grasp the tremendous implications of His exalted station and to more ardently admire and love Him.

There can be no doubt that the claim to the twofold station ordained for the Báb by the Almighty, a claim which He Himself has so boldly advanced, which Bahá'u'lláh has repeatedly affirmed, and to which the Will and Testament of 'Abdu'l-Bahá has finally given the sanction of its testimony, constitutes the most distinctive feature of the Bahá'í Dispensation. It is a further evidence of its uniqueness, a tremendous accession to the strength, to the mysterious power and authority with which this holy cycle has been invested. Indeed the greatness of the Báb consists primarily, not in His being the divinely-appointed Forerunner of so transcendent a Revelation, but rather in His having been invested with the powers inherent in the inaugurator of a separate religious Dispensation, and in His wielding, to a degree unrivaled by the Messengers gone before Him, the scepter of independent Prophethood.

The short duration of His Dispensation, the restricted range within which His laws and ordinances have been made to operate, supply no criterion whatever wherewith to judge its Divine origin and to evaluate the potency of its message. '*That so brief a span*', Bahá'u'lláh Himself explains, '*should have separated this most mighty and wondrous Revelation from Mine own previous Manifestation, is a secret that no man can unravel and a mystery such as no mind can fathom. Its duration had been foreordained, and no man shall ever discover its reason unless and until he be informed of the contents of My Hidden Book.*' '*Behold*,' Bahá'u'lláh further explains in the Kitáb-i-Badí', one of His works refuting the arguments of the people of the Bayán, '*behold, how immediately upon the completion of the ninth year of this wondrous, this most holy and merciful Dispensation, the requisite number of pure, of wholly consecrated and sanctified souls had been most secretly consummated.*'

The marvelous happenings that have heralded the advent of the Founder of the Bábí Dispensation, the dramatic circumstances of His own eventful life, the miraculous tragedy of His martyrdom, the magic of His influence exerted on the most eminent and powerful among His countrymen, to all of which every chapter of Nabíl's stirring narrative testifies, should in themselves be regarded as sufficient evidence of the validity of His claim to so exalted a station among the Prophets.

However graphic the record which the eminent chronicler of His life has transmitted to posterity, so luminous a narrative must pale before the glowing tribute paid to the Báb by the pen of Bahá'u'lláh. This tribute the Báb Himself has, by the clear assertion of His claim, abundantly supported, while the written testimonies of 'Abdu'l-Bahá have powerfully reinforced its character and elucidated its meaning.

Where else if not in the Kitáb-i-Íqán can the student of the Bábí Dispensation seek to find those affirmations that unmistakably attest the power and spirit which no man, except he be a Manifestation of God, can manifest? *'Could such a thing'*, exclaims Bahá'u'lláh, *'be made manifest except through the power of a Divine Revelation and the potency of God's invincible Will? By the righteousness of God! Were any one to entertain so great a Revelation in his heart the thought of such a declaration would alone confound him! Were the hearts of all men to be crowded into his heart, he would still hesitate to venture upon so awful an enterprise.'* *'No eye'*, He in another passage affirms, *'hath beheld so great an outpouring of bounty, nor hath any ear heard of such a Revelation of loving-kindness . . . The Prophets "endowed with constancy", whose loftiness and glory shine as the sun, were each honored with a Book which all have seen, and the verses of which have been duly ascertained. Whereas the verses which have rained from this Cloud of divine mercy have been so abundant that none hath yet been able to estimate their number . . . How can they belittle this Revelation? Hath any age witnessed such momentous happenings?'*

Commenting on the character and influence of those heroes and martyrs whom the spirit of the Báb had so magically transformed Bahá'u'lláh reveals the following: *'If these companions be not the true strivers after God, who else could be called by this name? . . . If these companions, with all their marvelous testimonies and wondrous works, be false, who then is worthy to claim for himself the truth? . . . Has the world since the days of Adam witnessed such tumult, such violent commotion? . . . Methinks, patience was revealed only by virtue of their fortitude, and faithfulness itself was begotten only by their deeds.'*

Wishing to stress the sublimity of the Báb's exalted station as compared with that of the Prophets of the past, Bahá'u'lláh in that same epistle asserts: *'No understanding can grasp the nature of His Revelation, nor can any knowledge comprehend the full measure of His Faith.'* He then quotes, in confirmation of His argument, these prophetic words: *'Knowledge is twenty and seven letters. All that the Prophets have revealed are two letters thereof. No man thus far hath known more than these two letters. But when the Qá'im shall arise, He will cause the remaining twenty and five letters to be made manifest.'* *'Behold,'* He adds, *'how great and lofty is His station! His rank excelleth that of all the Prophets and His Revelation transcendeth the comprehension and understanding of all their chosen ones.'* *'Of His Revelation'*, He further adds, *'the Prophets of God, His saints and chosen ones, have either not been informed, or, in pursuance of God's inscrutable decree, they have not disclosed.'*

Of all the tributes which Bahá'u'lláh's unerring pen has chosen to pay to the memory of the Báb, His 'Best-Beloved,' the most memorable and touching is this brief, yet eloquent passage which so greatly enhances the value of the concluding passages of that same epistle. *'Amidst them all,'* He writes, referring to the afflictive trials and dangers besetting Him in the city of Baghdád, *'We stand life in hand wholly resigned to His Will, that perchance through God's loving kindness and grace, this revealed and manifest Letter* (Bahá'u'lláh) *may lay down His life as a sacrifice in the path of the Primal Point, the most exalted Word* (the Báb). *By Him, at Whose bidding the Spirit hath spoken, but for this yearning of Our soul, We would not, for one moment, have tarried any longer in this city.'*

Dearly-beloved friends! So resounding a praise, so bold an assertion issued by the pen of Bahá'u'lláh in so weighty a work, are fully re-echoed in the language in which the Source of the Bábí Revelation has chosen to clothe the claims He Himself has advanced. *'I am the Mystic Fane'*, the Báb thus proclaims His station in the Qayyúmu'l-Asmá', *'which the Hand of Omnipotence hath reared. I am the Lamp which the Finger of God hath lit within its niche and caused to shine with deathless splendor. I am the Flame of that supernal Light that glowed upon Sinai in the gladsome Spot, and lay concealed in the midst of the Burning Bush.'* *'O Qurratu'l-'Ayn!'* He, addressing Himself in that same commentary, exclaims, *'I recognize in Thee none other except the "Great Announcement" – the Announcement voiced by the Concourse on high. By this name, I bear witness, they that circle the Throne of Glory have ever known Thee.'* *'With each and every Prophet, Whom We have sent down in the past,'* He further adds, *'We have established a separate Covenant concerning the "Remembrance of God" and His Day. Manifest, in the realm of glory and through the power of truth, are the "Remembrance of God" and His Day before the eyes of the angels that circle His mercy-seat.'* *'Should it be Our wish,'* He again affirms, *'it is in Our power to compel, through the agency of but one letter of Our Revelation, the world and all that is therein to recognize, in less than the twinkling of an eye, the truth of Our Cause.'*

'I am the Primal Point', the Báb thus addresses Muḥammad Sháh from the prison-fortress of Máh-Kú, *'from which have been generated all created things . . . I am the Countenance of God Whose splendor can never be obscured, the light of God whose radiance can never fade . . . All the keys of heaven God hath chosen to place on My right hand, and all the keys of hell on My left . . . I am one of the sustaining pillars of the Primal Word of God. Whosoever hath recognized*

Me, hath known all that is true and right, and hath attained all that is good and seemly . . . The substance wherewith God hath created Me is not the clay out of which others have been formed. He hath conferred upon Me that which the worldly-wise can never comprehend, nor the faithful discover.' 'Should a tiny ant', the Báb, wishing to stress the limitless potentialities latent in His Dispensation, characteristically affirms, *'desire in this day to be possessed of such power as to be able to unravel the abstrusest and most bewildering passages of the Qur'án, its wish will no doubt be fulfilled, inasmuch as the mystery of eternal might vibrates within the innermost being of all created things.'* 'If so helpless a creature,' is 'Abdu'l-Bahá's comment on so startling an affirmation, *'can be endowed with so subtle a capacity, how much more efficacious must be the power released through the liberal effusions of the grace of Bahá'u'lláh!'*

To these authoritative assertions and solemn declarations made by Bahá'u'lláh and the Báb must be added 'Abdu'l-Bahá's own incontrovertible testimony. He, the appointed interpreter of the utterances of both Bahá'u'lláh and the Báb, corroborates, not by implication but in clear and categorical language, both in His Tablets and in His Testament, the truth of the statements to which I have already referred.

In a Tablet addressed to a Bahá'í in Mázindarán, in which He unfolds the meaning of a misinterpreted statement attributed to Him regarding the rise of the Sun of Truth in this century, He sets forth, briefly but conclusively, what should remain for all time our true conception of the relationship between the two Manifestations associated with the Bahá'í Dispensation. *'In making such a statement,'* He explains, *'I had in mind no one else except the Báb and Bahá'u'lláh, the character of whose Revelations it had been my purpose to elucidate. The Revelation of the Báb may be likened to the sun, its station corresponding to the first sign of the Zodiac – the sign Aries – which the sun enters at the Vernal Equinox. The station of Bahá'u'lláh's Revelation, on the other hand, is represented by the sign Leo, the sun's mid-summer and highest station. By this is meant that this holy Dispensation is illumined with the light of the Sun of Truth shining from its most exalted station, and in the plenitude of its resplendency, its heat and glory.'*

'*The Báb, the Exalted One,*' 'Abdu'l-Bahá more specifically affirms in another Tablet, '*is the Morn of Truth, the splendor of Whose light shineth throughout all regions. He is also the Harbinger of the Most Great Light, the Abhá Luminary. The Blessed Beauty is the One promised by the sacred books of the past, the revelation of the Source of light that shone upon Mount Sinai, Whose fire glowed in the midst of the Burning Bush. We are, one and all, servants of their threshold, and stand each as a lowly keeper at their door.*' '*Every proof and prophecy,*' is His still more emphatic warning, '*every manner of evidence, whether based on reason or on the text of the scriptures and traditions, are to be regarded as centred in the persons of Bahá'u'lláh and the Báb. In them is to be found their complete fulfillment.*'

And finally, in His Will and Testament, the repository of His last wishes and parting instructions, He in the following passage, specifically designed to set forth the guiding principles of Bahá'í belief, sets the seal of His testimony on the Báb's dual and exalted station: '*The foundation of the belief of the people of Bahá (may my life be offered up for them) is this: His holiness the exalted One* (the Báb) *is the Manifestation of the unity and oneness of God and the Forerunner of the Ancient Beauty* (Bahá'u'lláh). *His holiness, the Abhá Beauty* (Bahá'u'lláh) *(may my life be offered up as a sacrifice for His steadfast friends) is the supreme Manifestation of God and the*

Day-Spring of His most divine Essence.' 'All others,' He significantly adds, '*are servants unto Him and do His bidding.*'[28]

❦

Not only in the character of the revelation of Bahá'u'lláh, however stupendous be His claim, does the greatness of this Dispensation reside. For among the distinguishing features of His Faith ranks, as a further evidence of its uniqueness, the fundamental truth that in the person of its Forerunner, the Báb, every follower of Bahá'u'lláh recognizes not merely an inspired annunciator but a direct Manifestation of God. It is their firm belief that, no matter how short the duration of His Dispensation, and however brief the period of the operation of His laws, the Báb had been endowed with a potency such as no founder of any of the past religions was, in the providence of the Almighty, allowed to possess. That He was not merely the precursor of the Revelation of Bahá'u'lláh, that He was more than a divinely-inspired personage, that His was the station of an independent, self-sufficient Manifestation of God, is abundantly demonstrated by Himself, is affirmed in unmistakable terms by Bahá'u'lláh, and is finally attested by the Will and Testament of 'Abdu'l-Bahá.

Nowhere but in the Kitáb-i-Íqán, Bahá'u'lláh's masterly exposition of the one unifying truth underlying all the Revelations of the past, can we obtain a clearer apprehension of the potency of those forces inherent in that Preliminary Manifestation with which His own Faith stands indissolubly associated. Expatiating upon the unfathomed import of the signs and tokens that have accompanied the Revelation proclaimed by the Báb, the promised Qá'im, He recalls these prophetic words: '*Knowledge is twenty and seven letters. All that the Prophets have revealed are two letters thereof. No man thus far hath known more than these two letters. But when the Qá'im shall arise, He will cause the remaining twenty and five letters to be made manifest.'* 'Behold,' adds Bahá'u'lláh, '*how great and lofty is His station!*' '*Of His Revelation,*' He further adds, '*the Prophets of God, His saints and chosen ones, have either not been informed, or in pursuance of God's inscrutable Decree, they have not disclosed.*'²⁹

ᥱᥣ

Moved to share with assembled representatives of American Bahá'í Community gathered beneath the dome of the Most Holy House of Worship in the Bahá'í world, feelings of profound emotion evoked by this historic occasion of the world-wide commemoration of the First Centenary of the Martyrdom of the Blessed Báb, Prophet and Herald of the Faith of Bahá'u'lláh, Founder of the Dispensation marking the culmination of the six thousand year old Adamic Cycle, Inaugurator of the five thousand century Bahá'í Cycle.

Poignantly call to mind the circumstances attending the last act consummating the tragic ministry of the Master-Hero of the most sublime drama in the religious annals of mankind, signalizing the most dramatic event of the most turbulent period of the Heroic Age of the Bahá'í Dispensation, destined to be recognized by posterity as the most precious, momentous sacrifice in the world's spiritual history. Recall the peerless tributes paid to His memory by the Founder of the Faith, acclaiming Him Monarch of God's Messengers, the Primal Point round Whom the realities of all the Prophets circle in adoration. Profoundly stirred by the memory of the agonies He suffered, the glad-tidings He announced, the warnings He uttered, the forces

He set in motion, the adversaries He converted, the disciples He raised up, the conflagrations He precipitated, the legacy He left of faith and courage, the love He inspired. Acknowledge with bowed head, joyous, thankful heart the successive, marvelous evidence of His triumphant power in the course of the hundred years elapsed since the last crowning act of His meteoric ministry.

The creative energies released at the hour of the birth of His Revelation, endowing mankind with the potentialities of the attainment of maturity are deranging, during the present transitional age, the equilibrium of the entire planet as the inevitable prelude to the consummation in world unity of the coming of age of the human race. The portentous but unheeded warnings addressed to kings, princes, ecclesiastics are responsible for the successive overthrow of fourteen monarchies of East and West, the collapse of the institution of the Caliphate, the virtual extinction of the Pope's temporal sovereignty, the progressive decline in the fortunes of the ecclesiastical hierarchies of the Islámic, Christian, Jewish, Zoroastrian, and Hindu Faiths.

The Order eulogized and announced in His writings, whose laws Bahá'u'lláh subsequently revealed in the Most Holy Book, whose features 'Abdu'l-Bahá delineated in His Testament, is now passing through its embryonic stage through the emergence of the initial institutions of the world Administrative Order in the five continents of the globe. The clarion call sounded in the Qayyúmu'l-Asmá', summoning the peoples of the West to forsake their homes and proclaim His message, was nobly answered by the communities of the Western Hemisphere headed by the valorous, stalwart American believers, the chosen vanguard of the all-conquering, irresistibly marching army of the Faith in the western world.

The embryonic Faith, maturing three years after His

martyrdom, traversing the period of infancy in the course
of the Heroic Age of the Faith is now steadily progressing
towards maturity in the present Formative Age, destined
to attain full stature in the Golden Age of the Bahá'í
Dispensation.

Lastly the Holy Seed of infinite preciousness, holding
within itself incalculable potentialities representing the
culmination of the centuries-old process of the evolution
of humanity through the energies released by the series of
progressive Revelations starting with Adam and concluded
by the Revelation of the Seal of the Prophets, marked by
the successive appearance of the branches, leaves, buds,
blossoms and plucked, after six brief years by the hand of
destiny, ground in the mill of martyrdom and oppression
but yielding the oil whose first flickering light cast upon
the somber, subterranean walls of the Síyáh-Chál of Ṭihrán,
whose fire gathered brilliance in Baghdád and shone in
full resplendency in its crystal globe in Adrianople, whose
rays warmed and illuminated the fringes of the American,
European, Australian continents through the tender min-
isterings of the Center of the Covenant, whose radiance
is now overspreading the surface of the globe during the
present Formative Age, whose full splendor is destined in
the course of future milleniums to suffuse the entire planet.

Already the crushing of this God-imbued kernel upon
the anvil of adversity has ignited the first sparks of the Holy
Fire latent within it through the emergence of the firmly
knit world-encompassing community constituting no less
than twenty-five hundred centers established throughout a
hundred countries representing over thirty races and extend-
ing as far north as the Arctic Circle and as far south as the
Straits of Magallanes, equipped with literature translated
into sixty languages and possessing endowments nearing

ten million dollars, enriched through the erection of two Houses of Worship in the heart of the Asiatic and North American continents and the stately mausoleum reared in its World Center, consolidated through the incorporation of over a hundred of its national and local assemblies and reinforced through the proclamation of its independence in the East, its recognition in the West, eulogized by royalty, buttressed by nine pillars sustaining the future structure of its supreme administrative council, energized through the simultaneous prosecution of specific plans conducted under the aegis of its national councils designed to enlarge the limits and extend the ramifications and consolidate the foundations of its divinely appointed Administrative Order over the surface of the entire planet.[30]

4

EXTRACTS FROM BÁBÍ AND BAHÁ'Í AUTHORS

Extracts from Bábí and Baháʼí authors

On May 22nd, 1844, a young merchant of S̲h̲íráz, whose name was Siyyid ʻAlí Muḥammad, revealed Himself to a seeker as that Deliverer Whom the world of Islám anxiously awaited. An independent Manifestation of God and the Harbinger of a greater Manifestation, He took the title of the Báb, meaning 'Gate'. His primary mission was to awaken the slumbering people of Írán, and to warn the followers of the Faith of Muḥammad – a Faith by then, alas, laden with abuses.[31]

Hasan Balyuzi

ᘓ

Mírzá Aḥmad-i-Qazvíní, the martyr, who on several occasions had heard Mullá Ḥusayn recount to the early believers the story of his moving and historic interview with the Báb, related to me the following: 'I have heard Mullá Ḥusayn repeatedly and graphically describe the circumstances of that remarkable interview: "The Youth who met me outside the gate of S̲h̲íráz overwhelmed me with expressions of affection and loving-kindness. He extended to me a warm invitation to visit His home, and there refresh myself after the fatigues of my journey. I prayed to be excused, pleading that my two companions had already arranged for my stay in that city, and were now awaiting my return. 'Commit them to the care of God,' was His reply; 'He will surely protect and watch over them.' Having spoken these words, He bade me follow Him. I was profoundly impressed by the gentle yet compelling manner in which that strange Youth spoke to me. As I followed Him, His gait, the charm of His voice, the dignity of His bearing, served to enhance my first impressions of this unexpected meeting.

'"We soon found ourselves standing at the gate of a house of modest appearance. He knocked at the door, which was soon opened by an Ethiopian servant. 'Enter therein in peace, secure,' were His words as He crossed the threshold and motioned me to follow Him. His invitation, uttered with power and majesty, penetrated my soul. I thought it a good augury to be addressed in such words, standing as I did on the threshold of the first house I was entering in Shíráz, a city the very atmosphere of which had produced already an indescribable impression upon me. Might not my visit to this house, I thought to myself, enable me to draw nearer to the Object of my quest? Might it not hasten the termination of a period of intense longing, of strenuous search, of increasing anxiety, which such a quest involves? As I entered the house and followed my Host to His chamber, a feeling of unutterable joy invaded my being. Immediately we were seated, He ordered a ewer of water to be brought, and bade me wash away from my hands and feet the stains of travel. I pleaded permission to retire from His presence and perform my ablutions in an adjoining room. He refused to grant my request, and proceeded to pour the water over my hands. He then gave me to drink of a refreshing beverage, after which He asked for the samovar and Himself prepared the tea which He offered me.

'"Overwhelmed with His acts of extreme kindness, I arose to depart. 'The time for evening prayer is approaching,' I ventured to observe. 'I have promised my friends to join them at that hour in the Masjid-i-Ílkhání.' With extreme courtesy and calm He replied: 'You must surely have made the hour of your return conditional upon the will and pleasure of God. It seems that His will has decreed otherwise. You need have no fear of having broken your pledge.' His dignity and self-assurance silenced me I renewed my ablutions and prepared for prayer. He, too, stood beside me and prayed. Whilst praying, I unburdened my soul, which was much oppressed, both by the mystery of this interview and the strain and stress of my search. I breathed this prayer: 'I have striven with all my soul, O my God, and until now have failed to find Thy promised Messenger. I testify that Thy word faileth not, and that Thy promise is sure.'

'"That night, that memorable night, was the eve preceding the fifth day of Jamádíyu'l-Avval, in the year 1260 A.H. It was about an hour after sunset when my youthful Host began to converse with me. 'Whom, after Siyyid Kázim,' He asked me, 'do you regard as his successor and your leader?' 'At the hour of his death,' I replied, 'our departed teacher insistently exhorted us to forsake our homes, to scatter far and wide, in quest of the promised Beloved. I have, accordingly, journeyed to Persia, have arisen to accomplish his will, and am still engaged in my quest.' 'Has your teacher,' He further enquired, 'given you any detailed indications as to the distinguishing features of the promised One?' 'Yes,' I replied, 'He is of a pure lineage, is of illustrious descent, and of the seed of Fátimih. As to His age, He is more than twenty and less than thirty. He is endowed with innate knowledge. He is of medium height, abstains from smoking, and is free from bodily deficiency.' He paused for a while and then with vibrant voice declared: 'Behold, all these signs are manifest in Me!' He then considered each of the above-mentioned signs separately, and conclusively demonstrated that each and all were applicable to His person. I was greatly surprised, and politely observed: 'He whose advent we await is a Man of unsurpassed holiness, and the Cause He is to reveal, a Cause of tremendous power. Many and diverse are the requirements which He who claims to be its visible embodiment must needs fulfil. How often has Siyyid Kázim referred to the vastness of the knowledge of the promised One! How often did he say: "My own knowledge is but a drop compared with that with which He has been endowed. All my attainments are but a speck of dust in the face of the immensity of His knowledge. Nay, immeasurable is the difference!"' No sooner had those words dropped from my lips than I found myself seized with fear and remorse, such as I could neither conceal nor explain. I bitterly reproved myself, and resolved at that very moment to alter my attitude and to soften my tone. I vowed to God that should my Host again refer to the subject, I would, with the utmost humility, answer and say: 'If you be willing to substantiate your claim, you will most assuredly deliver me from the anxiety and suspense which so heavily oppress my soul. I shall truly be indebted to you for such deliverance.' When I first started upon my quest, I determined to regard the two following standards as those whereby I could ascertain the truth of whosoever might claim to be the promised Qá'im. The first was a treatise which I had myself composed, bearing upon the abstruse and hidden teachings propounded by Shaykh Ahmad and Siyyid Kázim. Whoever seemed to me capable of unravelling the mysterious allusions made in that treatise, to him I would next submit my second request, and would ask him to reveal, without the least hesitation or reflection, a commentary on the Súrih of Joseph, in a style and language entirely different from the prevailing standards of the time. I had previously requested Siyyid Kázim, in private, to write a commentary on that same Súrih, which he refused, saying: 'This is, verily, beyond me. He, that great One, who comes after me will, unasked, reveal it for you. That commentary will constitute one of the weightiest testimonies of

His truth, and one of the clearest evidences of the loftiness of His position.'

'"I was revolving these things in my mind, when my distinguished Host again remarked: 'Observe attentively. Might not the Person intended by Siyyid Káẓim be none other than I?' I thereupon felt impelled to present to Him a copy of the treatise which I had with me. 'Will you,' I asked Him, 'read this book of mine and look at its pages with indulgent eyes? I pray you to overlook my weaknesses and failings.' He graciously complied with my wish. He opened the book, glanced at certain passages, closed it, and began to address me. Within a few minutes He had, with characteristic vigour and charm, unravelled all its mysteries and resolved all its problems. Having to my entire satisfaction accomplished, within so short a time, the task I had expected Him to perform, He further expounded to me certain truths which could be found neither in the reported sayings of the imáms of the Faith nor in the writings of Shaykh Aḥmad and Siyyid Káẓim. These truths, which I had never heard before, seemed to be endowed with refreshing vividness and power. 'Had you not been My guest,' He afterwards observed, 'your position would indeed have been a grievous one. The all-encompassing grace of God has saved you. It is for God to test His servants, and not for His servants to judge Him in accordance with their deficient standards. Were I to fail to resolve your perplexities, could the Reality that shines within Me be regarded as powerless, or My knowledge be accused as faulty? Nay, by the righteousness of God! it behoves, in this day, the peoples and nations of both the East and the West to hasten to this threshold, and here seek to obtain the reviving grace of the Merciful. Whoso hesitates will indeed be in grievous loss. Do not the peoples of the earth testify that the fundamental purpose of their creation is the knowledge and adoration of God? It behoves them to arise, as earnestly and spontaneously as you have arisen, and to seek with determination and constancy their promised Beloved.' He then proceeded to say: 'Now is the time to reveal the commentary on the Súrih of Joseph.' He took up His pen and with incredible rapidity revealed the entire Súrih of Mulk, the first chapter of His commentary on the Súrih of Joseph. The overpowering effect of the manner in which He wrote was heightened by the gentle intonation of His voice which accompanied His writing. Not for one moment did He interrupt the flow of the verses which streamed from His pen. Not once did He pause till the Súrih of Mulk was finished. I sat enraptured by the magic of His voice and the sweeping force of His revelation. At last I reluctantly arose from my seat and begged leave to depart. He smilingly bade me be seated, and said: 'If you leave in such a state, whoever sees you will assuredly say: "This poor youth has lost his mind."' At that moment the clock registered two hours and eleven minutes after sunset. That night, the eve of the fifth day of Jamádiyu'l-Avval, in the year 1260 A.H., corresponded with the eve preceding the sixty-fifth day after Naw-rúz, which was also the eve of the sixth day of Khurdád, of the year Nahang. 'This night,' He declared, 'this very hour will, in the days to come, be celebrated as one of the greatest and most significant of all festivals. Render thanks to God for having graciously assisted you to attain your heart's desire, and for having quaffed from the sealed wine of His utterance. "Well is it with them that attain thereunto."'

'"At the third hour after sunset, my Host ordered the dinner to be served. That same Ethiopian servant appeared again and spread before us the choicest food. That holy repast refreshed alike my body and soul. In the presence of my Host, at that hour, I felt as though I were feeding upon the fruits of Paradise. I could not but marvel at the manners and the devoted attentions of that Ethiopian servant whose very life seemed to have been transformed by the regenerating influence of his Master. I then, for the first time, recognized the significance of this well-known traditional utterance ascribed to Muḥammad: 'I have prepared for the godly and righteous among My servants what eye hath seen not, ear heard not, nor human heart conceived.' Had my youthful Host no other claim to greatness, this were sufficient – that He received me with that quality of hospitality and loving-kindness which I was convinced no other human being could possibly reveal.

'"I sat spellbound by His utterance, oblivious of time and of those who awaited me. Suddenly the call of the muadhdhín, summoning the faithful to their morning prayer, awakened me from the state of ecstasy into which I seemed to have fallen. All the delights, all the ineffable glories, which the Almighty has recounted in His Book as the priceless possessions of the people of Paradise – these I seemed to be experiencing that night. Methinks I was in a place of which it could be truly said: 'Therein no toil shall reach us, and therein no weariness shall touch us'; 'No vain discourse shall they hear therein, nor any falsehood, but only the cry, "Peace! Peace!"'; 'Their cry therein shall be, "Glory be to Thee, O God!" and their salutation therein, "Peace!" And the close of their cry, "Praise be to God, Lord of all creatures!"'

'"Sleep had departed from me that night. I was enthralled by the music of that voice which rose and fell as He chanted; now swelling forth as He revealed verses of the Qayyúmu'l-Asmá', again acquiring ethereal, subtle harmonies as He uttered the prayers He was revealing. At the end of each invocation, He would repeat this verse: 'Far from the glory of thy Lord, the All-Glorious, be that which His creatures affirm of Him! And peace be upon His Messengers! And praise be to God, the Lord of all beings!'

'"He then addressed me in these words: 'O thou who art the first to believe in Me! Verily I say, I am the Báb, the Gate of God, and thou art the Bábu'l-Báb, the gate of that Gate. Eighteen souls must, in the beginning, spontaneously and of their own accord, accept Me and recognize the truth of My Revelation. Unwarned and uninvited, each of these must seek independently to find Me. And when their number is complete, one of them must needs be chosen to accompany Me on My pilgrimage to Mecca and Medina. There I shall deliver the Message of God to the Sharíf of Mecca. I then shall return to Kúfih, where again, in the Masjid of that holy city, I shall manifest His Cause. It is incumbent upon you not to divulge, either to your companions or to any other soul, that which you have seen and heard. Be engaged in the Masjid-i-Ílkhání in prayer and in teaching. I, too, will there join you in congregational prayer. Beware lest your attitude towards Me betray the secret of your faith. You should continue in this occupation and maintain this attitude until our departure for Hijáz. Ere we depart, we shall appoint unto each of the eighteen souls his special mission, and shall send them forth to accomplish their task. We shall instruct them to teach the Word of God and to quicken the souls of men.' Having spoken these words to me, He dismissed me from His presence. Accompanying me to the door of the house, He committed me to the care of God.

'"This Revelation, so suddenly and impetuously thrust upon me, came as a thunderbolt which, for a time, seemed to have benumbed my faculties. I was blinded by its dazzling splendour and overwhelmed by its crushing force.

Excitement, joy, awe, and wonder stirred the depths of my soul. Predominant among these emotions was a sense of gladness and strength which seemed to have transfigured me. How feeble and impotent, how dejected and timid, I had felt previously! Then I could neither write nor walk, so tremulous were my hands and feet. Now, however, the knowledge of His Revelation had galvanised my being. I felt possessed of such courage and power that were the world, all its peoples and its potentates, to rise against me, I would, alone and undaunted, withstand their onslaught. The universe seemed but a handful of dust in my grasp. I seemed to be the Voice of Gabriel personified, calling unto all mankind: 'Awake, for lo! the morning Light has broken. Arise, for His Cause is made manifest. The portal of His grace is open wide; enter therein, O peoples of the world! For He who is your promised One is come!'"'[32]

Nabíl-i-A'ẓam

Shaykh Ḥasan-i-Zunúzí, himself, informed me that he too entertained such doubts, that he prayed to God that if his supposition was well founded he should be confirmed in his belief, and if not that he should be delivered from such idle fancy. 'I was so perturbed,' he once related to me, 'that for days I could neither eat nor sleep. My days were spent in the service of Siyyid Káẓim, to whom I was greatly attached. One day, at the hour of dawn, I was suddenly awakened by Mullá Naw-rúz, one of his intimate attendants, who, in great excitement, bade me arise and follow him. We went to the house of Siyyid Káẓim, where we found him fully dressed, wearing his 'abá, and ready to leave his home. He asked me to accompany him. "A highly esteemed and distinguished Person," he said, "has arrived. I feel it incumbent upon us both to visit Him." The morning light had just broken when I found myself walking with him through the streets of Karbilá. We soon reached a house, at the door of which stood a Youth, as if expectant to receive us. He wore a green turban, and His countenance revealed an expression of humility and kindliness which I can never describe. He quietly approached us, extended His arms towards Siyyid Kázim, and lovingly embraced him. His affability and loving-kindness singularly contrasted with the sense of profound reverence that characterized the attitude of Siyyid Kázim towards him. Speechless and with bowed head, he received the many expressions of affection and esteem with which that Youth greeted him. We were soon led by Him to the upper floor of that house, and entered a chamber bedecked with flowers and redolent of the loveliest perfume. He bade us be seated. We knew not, however, what seats we actually occupied, so overpowering was the sense of delight which seized us. We observed a silver cup which had been placed in the centre of the room, which our youthful Host, soon after we were seated, filled to overflowing, and handed to Siyyid Kázim, saying: "A drink of a pure beverage shall their Lord give them." Siyyid Kázim held the cup with both hands and quaffed it. A feeling of reverent joy filled his being, a feeling which he could not suppress. I too was presented with a cupful of that beverage, though no words were addressed to me. All that was spoken at that memorable gathering was the above-mentioned verse of the Qur'án. Soon after, the Host arose from His seat and, accompanying us to the threshold of the house, bade us farewell. I was mute with wonder, and knew not how to express the cordiality of His welcome, the dignity of His bearing, the charm of that face, and the delicious fragrance of that beverage. How great was my amazement when I saw my teacher quaff without the least hesitation that holy draught from a silver cup, the use of which, according to the precepts of Islám, is forbidden to the faithful. I could not explain the motive which could have induced the Siyyid to manifest such profound reverence in the presence of that Youth – a reverence which even the sight of the shrine of the Siyyidu'sh-Shuhadá' had failed to excite. Three days later, I saw that same Youth arrive and take His seat in the midst of the company of the assembled disciples of Siyyid Kázim. He sat close to the threshold, and with the same modesty and dignity of bearing listened to the discourse of the Siyyid. As soon as his eyes fell upon that Youth, the Siyyid discontinued his address and held his peace. Whereupon one of his disciples begged him to resume the argument which he had left unfinished. "What more shall I say?" replied Siyyid Kázim, as he turned his face toward the Báb. "Lo, the Truth is more manifest than the ray of light that has fallen upon that lap!" I immediately observed that the ray to which the Siyyid referred had fallen upon the lap of that same Youth whom we had recently visited. "Why is it," that questioner enquired, "that you neither reveal His name nor identify His person?" To this the Siyyid replied by pointing with his finger to his own throat, implying that were he to divulge His name, they both would be put to death instantly. This added still further to my perplexity. I had already heard my teacher observe that so great is the perversity of this generation, that were he to point with his finger to the promised One and say: "He indeed is the Beloved, the Desire of your hearts and mine," they would still fail to recognize and acknowledge Him. I saw the Siyyid actually point out with his finger the ray of light that had fallen on that lap, and yet none among those who were present seemed to apprehend its meaning. I, for my part, was convinced that the Siyyid himself could never be the promised One, but that a mystery inscrutable to us all, lay concealed in that strange and attractive Youth. Several times I ventured to approach Siyyid Káẓim and seek from him an elucidation of this mystery. Every time I approached him, I was overcome by a sense of awe which his personality so powerfully inspired. Many a time I heard him remark: "O Shaykh Ḥasan, rejoice that your name is Ḥasan [praiseworthy]; Ḥasan your beginning, and Ḥasan your end. You have been privileged to attain to the day of Shaykh Aḥmad, you have been closely associated with me, and in the days to come yours shall be the inestimable joy of beholding 'what eye hath seen not, ear heard not, nor any heart conceived.'"

'I often felt the urge to seek alone the presence of that Háshimite Youth and to endeavour to fathom His mystery. I watched Him several times as He stood in an attitude of prayer at the doorway of the shrine of the Imám Ḥusayn. So wrapt was He in His devotions that He seemed utterly oblivious of those around Him. Tears rained from His eyes, and from His lips fell words of glorification and praise of such power and beauty as even the noblest passages of our sacred Scriptures could not hope to surpass. The words "O God, my God, my Beloved, my heart's Desire" were uttered with a frequency and ardour that those of the visiting pilgrims who were near enough to hear Him instinctively interrupted the course of their devotions, and marvelled at the evidences of piety and veneration which that youthful countenance evinced. Like Him they were moved to tears, and from Him they learned the lesson of true adoration. Having completed His prayers, that Youth, without crossing the threshold of the shrine and without attempting to

address any words to those around Him, would quietly
return to His home. I felt the impulse to address Him, but
every time I ventured an approach, a force that I could
neither explain nor resist, detained me. My enquiries about
Him elicited the information that He was a resident of
Shíráz, that He was a merchant by profession, and did not
belong to any of the ecclesiastical orders. I was, moreover,
informed that He, and also His uncles and relatives, were
among the lovers and admirers of Shaykh Aḥmad and
Siyyid Káẓim. Soon after, I learned that He had departed
for Najaf on His way to Shíráz. That Youth had set my heart
aflame. The memory of that vision haunted me. My soul
was wedded to His till the day when the call of a Youth from
Shíráz, proclaiming Himself to be the Báb, reached my ears.
The thought instantly flashed through my mind that such a
person could be none other than that selfsame Youth whom
I had seen in Karbilá, the Youth of my heart's desire.'³³

Nabíl-i-A'ẓam

℅

To these humble servants of the altar of the heart the Báb
revealed Himself in 1844. He was twenty-five years of age.
The Báb, His title meaning 'door' or 'gate,' exemplified
a radiance, a beauty of being and of person, a power of
spirit, a penetration of love which became the adoration of
a mighty host. In that darkened, ignorant, tyrannical land
the Báb arose as with the light of a dawning Sun. So powerful was He in quickening the human spirit, in establishing
the standard of reality dividing the people into believers and
non-believers, that within the span of six years His earthly
destiny was fulfilled. Condemned for heresy, denounced as
rebel, the Báb was imprisoned and executed in the city of

Tabríz. It was a time of profound spiritual experience. . . .

Every testimony reveals the splendour of that holy Dawn, when men of sincerity and truth attained the purpose of their being in becoming filled with a new spirit and a new life. They had full assurance that this was no personal and no local experience, but a new enlightenment and impetus for the regeneration of the world. In the Báb they touched the mystery of the oneness of God, and in His spiritual being they felt the presence of all the Prophets through whom God has been manifested in the past. The Báb restored the power of providence to human affairs. Against Him sped the arrows of bitterest ecclesiastical and civil rancour. The Báb was the chosen Victim by whose sacrifice the human spirit could be given life, and a new direction established for the course of man's spiritual and social evolution. . . .

In such pure sacrifice was opened the door of divine guidance, and the mission of the Báb initiated the release of forces and powers which since, with increasing intensity, have acted upon mankind.[34]

Horace Holley

౮

The origin of the Cause itself coincided in point of time with the beginnings of what all thoughtful people discern to be a new era in the development of mankind. Here in the West, the new era manifested itself most visibly through the abrupt industrial revolution produced by the influence of scientific discovery; in the East, less visibly, the same ferment and universal spirit of change also had its effects in the realm of feeling and thought. . . .

Between May 23rd, 1844, and July 9th, 1850, occurred

that remarkable series of events known to history as the 'Episode of the Báb.' Within the brief compass of six years a single youth had succeeded in shattering the age-long inertia of the country [Persia] and animating thousands of people with an intense, all-encompassing expectation of an imminent fulfillment of their profoundest religious belief. The teaching had been quietly spread even before the appearance of the Báb that the time had come for a new spiritual leader – one who should restore the foundations of faith and open the gates to an expression of universal truth. A survey of the religious experience of other peoples would reveal the working of the same influence here and there both in the East and the West at that time.

It was the presence of this quiet yet powerful undercurrent of hope that gave the Báb His commanding position among the people, for His teaching expressed their own inmost thought and gave vital substance to their secret dreams. The martyrdom of the Báb in 1850, consequently, was but the extinguishing of a torch which had already communicated its flame far and wide. To extinguish the flame itself proved impossible, though the annals of the world's religions contain no records of deliberate persecution more cruelly imposed, nor suffered voluntarily by so many believers.[35]

Horace Holley

ↄ

With the Báb the Kingdom actually begins. He stands both as a Revealer Prophet bringing His own Dispensation and Laws and also as a Forerunner of One, Bahá'u'lláh, bearing a Revelation immeasurably greater than His own. . . .

The creative energies which He imparts endow mankind

with the capacity to attain its maturity which will enable it in course of time and in conjunction with the still greater power generated by Bahá'u'lláh to achieve the organic unification of the human race.[36]

George Townshend

ಌ

Born October 20th, 1819, He was at the time of His Declaration a youth of twenty-five years of age. Of those eager active souls whom He quickly gathered about Him to raise the standard of the Cause of God, not a few were, like Himself, in the prime of their young manhood. Perhaps the flame of their youthfulness helped to animate the Bábí movement with that spirit of daring and adventure and indomitable courage which has helped to spread its fame far among the nations. Certainly the radiant charm and sweetness of its hero which made him seem Love's avatar, and that instinctive power which was His of drawing forth from all who opened to Him their hearts a passionate devotion which shrank from no sacrifice – certainly these qualities and the heinousness of the priestly hate that martyred him, have given to the brief sad chronicle of his career a tragic beauty which make it one of the most poignant episodes in the history of the religious world . . .

The teaching of the Báb, like His character, was beautiful and attractive; but His function of making ready a way for the advent of Bahá'u'lláh combined with the abject degradation of the Persian Church, made Him appear as in the first place a breaker of idols, an assailant of abuses, a remover of obsolete but cherished laws and traditions . . .

The reforms of the Báb challenged the corruptions and the hypocrisies of the time; and when His energetic measures rapidly spread his influence far and wide, the forces of the government were at once mobilised against him.[37]

George Townshend

〜

. . . (the saintly heroic figure of the Báb, a leader so mild and so serene, yet eager, resolute, and dominant; the devotion of His followers facing oppression with unbroken courage and often with ecstasy; the rage of a jealous priesthood inflaming for its own purpose the passions of a bloodthirsty populace) – these speak a language which all may understand. . . .

From the beginning the Báb must have divined the reception which would be accorded by His countrymen to His teachings, and the fate which awaited Him at the hands of the mullás. But He did not allow personal misgivings to affect the frank enunciation of His claims nor the open presentation of His Cause. The innovations which He proclaimed, though purely religious, were drastic; the announcement of His own identity startling and tremendous. He made Himself known as the Qá'im, the High Prophet or Messiah so long promised, so eagerly expected by the Muḥammadan world. He added to this the declaration that He was also the Gate (that is, the Báb) through Whom a greater Manifestation than Himself was to enter the human realm. . . .

His qualities were so rare in their nobility and beauty, His personality so gentle and yet so forceful, and His natural charm was combined with so much tact and judgment, that after His Declaration He quickly became in Persia a widely popular figure. He would win over almost all with whom He was brought into personal contact, often converting His gaolers to His Faith and turning the ill-disposed into admiring friends.[38]

George Townshend

ℰↃ

Here once again in human history is the Light shining in a darkness that comprehendeth it not! Here once again is Faith re-arisen upon the world, bringing a New Day, shedding a new glory, calling men from sleep to a new life.

Here once again is Religion that man had thought sunk for ever in impotence – religion in its freshness, its purity and its power, religion reborn with all the magic of that ancient sweetness and beauty with which it was clothed in Holy Writ of old – religion warming men's hearts with a new compassion and loving-kindness, melting all estrangements, uniting many wills in a common devotion, a common sympathy, giving to life a new completeness, transcending sorrow and pain and death!

We of the western world may be unable to trace in human affairs about us the providence of God, may not see His path opening before our feet, may not be aware of His activity and presence in our midst, we may be divided one against another, may be full of fears, devoid of love, laden with deepening doubt.

But here are men and women, boys and girls who through faith reborn became possessed of a knowledge to which we are strangers, entered into an experience which we hardly believe to exist, whose eyes were opened to the Light from heaven, who had ears to hear the voice of God, and being changed from their old selves, transformed into new creatures, translated to a new degree of life, were by divine grace endowed with a courage, an energy, a blissfulness which has no likeness on the earth and which no earthly privation can impair. . . .

Here once more is the Messenger of God, God's image mirrored in an all-perfect Love, God's power poured forth among men stirring them to a new spirituality, opening to them new reaches of consciousness. Here in very deed and in a form and fashion that none can gainsay or disown, is the vindication of the reality of religion, the proof of its present power in this modern world. Here is the re-affirmation of the dignity of human nature and of the infinite greatness of the purpose of human life. . . .

Here are men, women and children, a vast, motley, heterogeneous host of young and old, learned and unlearned, the rich man and the poor man, the aristocrat and the labourer: gathered into one indissoluble body not by any outward compulsion or constraint whatever, but of their own free act and eager choice. The tie that binds them is spiritual only – simply love for God – and is so strong that no enticement or repulsion of the earth can break or loosen it. Neither prison nor poverty, hunger nor thirst nor wounds could force them to desert their comrades, deny their Lord or abandon His cause: severally, or in multitudes together, they would face and welcome death, and give their lives, as their Beloved Lord gave His, simply to serve the cause of God among men.[39]

George Townshend

❧

Again and again He [the Báb] declared, both verbally and in writing, that the purpose of His Revelation was to prepare the way for 'Him Whom God shall make manifest,' upon Whose finger, He proclaimed, He was but as a ring. The Bábí and Bahá'í Faiths are two distinct religions, but the purpose of the Bábí Faith has been fulfilled and, in accordance with the Báb's own commands, virtually all the Bábís have become Bahá'ís. It is a sign of the greatness of this

Day that a Manifestation of God should have been sent as a Forerunner of Bahá'u'lláh to inaugurate a Dispensation that lasted only nine years.

The story of the Báb is indeed a fascinating one. Only 25 when He declared Himself to be from God, He possessed a charming personality, which attracted and overcame all who had dealings with Him. His cruel and corrupt opponents, backed by the power of the Church and State, were quite unable to resist the spread of His doctrines. Ever greater violence was used against the Bábís until at last, in desperation, little groups in different parts of the country withdrew to fortified positions to resist attack.

The heroism of these inspired defenders, mere handfuls who resisted for months whole armies, is already legendary; but in the course of the battles nearly all the Bábí leaders were slain. Eventually, the Báb Himself was condemned to death and shot in circumstances that would be incredible were they not so well attested . . .[40]

John Ferraby

∾

His Holiness the Báb had accomplished His Mission, under difficulties inexpressible, in bonds and imprisonment, steadfastly facing scorn, contempt, revilings. He had succeeded in establishing the conditions of purity of heart in many 'Waiting Servants,' who had become His devoted followers; this condition of heart being necessary in order to be able to recognize 'Him Whom God shall make Manifest'. . .

Through this 'Gate' the 'Waiting Servants' should pass, drawing with them the despairing, the humble and lowly of heart, those whose heads are adorned with the Crown of Severance from all things of earth, and those pure and holy ones, whose lives are made perfect through love.

For of such are the dwellers in the new Heaven, and the new earth.[41]

Sara Louisa, Lady Blomfield

⌘

'Báb' means 'Gate'! The Báb was the Gate to a new Kingdom – the Kingdom of God on earth . . .

The Báb was a great manifestation of God. In all His Writings He said that the main purpose of His coming was to give the glad-tidings that very soon the Promised One of all ages would appear. He warned His followers to beware lest they fail to recognize 'Him Whom God would make manifest.' He said that they should lay aside everything else and follow Him as soon as they heard His Message. The Báb wrote many prayers beseeching God that His own life might be accepted as a sacrifice to the Beloved of His heart, the One 'Whom God shall make manifest.' He even referred in His Writings to the Order of Bahá'u'lláh, and said: 'Well is it with him who follows Bahá'u'lláh.'

The Báb's prayers were answered and His promise was fulfilled. Nineteen years after His Mission, Bahá'u'lláh openly declared that He was the Promised One Whose coming had been foretold by all the Manifestations of God in past ages.[42]

Hushmand Fathe'azam

⌘

There is a glory of youth about the tragic mission of the Báb, which, from the human standpoint, is irresistible and compelling. He was but twenty-five years old when he gave his announcement that a new Day of God had dawned, a day of brotherhood and unity, when all men shall begin to love one another, a day of Manifestation, when men shall again learn to know God, 'and I am the Herald of this Day!'

Courageous and loving to a supreme degree, the spirit of God upon him seemed to enhance the splendour of his youth, to intensify the accent of his consecration. He was two years younger than Jesus when he gave His life in the same sacrifice for the salvation of the world, declaring himself the precursor of that wonderful second coming so long expected. The theologians have destroyed the beauty of youth in Jesus, but its radiance will always linger upon the Báb, Who will be remembered as a wonderful illumined boy going to martyrdom with a smile upon his lips![43]

Mary Hanford Ford

❧

So it is necessary not only to admit but to love and admire the Báb. Poor great Prophet, born in the heart of Persia, without any means of instruction, and who, alone in the world, encircled by enemies, succeeds by the force of his genius in creating a universal and wise religion . . . I want people to admire the sublimity of the Báb, who has, moreover, paid with his life, with his blood, for the reforms he preached. Cite me another similar example.[44]

A. L. M. Nicolas

❧

Dawnbreaker

Ablaze
with candles sconce
in weeping eyes
of wounds,

He danced
through jeering streets
to death; oh sang
against

The drumming
mockery God's praise.
Flames nested in
his flesh

Fed the
fires that consume
us now, the fire that
will save.[45]

Robert Hayden

5
ESSAYS

Essays

In this essay, first published in the 1994–95 edition of The Bahá'í World, *Douglas Martin considers the Revelation of the Báb in the context of its impact on the Western writers of the period and its subsequent influence.*

The Mission of the Báb: Retrospective, 1844–1944

The year 1994 marked the 150th anniversary of the declaration of His mission by the Báb (Siyyid 'Alí-Muḥammad, 1819–1850), one of the two Founders of the Bahá'í Faith. The moment invites an attempt to gain an overview of the extraordinary historical consequences that have flowed from an event little noticed at the time outside the confines of the remote and decadent society within which it occurred.

The first half of the nineteenth century was a period of messianic expectation in the Islamic world, as was the case in many parts of Christendom. In Persia a wave of millenialist enthusiasm had swept many in the religiously educated class of Shí'ih Muslim society, focused on belief that the fulfillment of prophecies in the Qur'án and the Islamic traditions was at hand. It was to one such ardent seeker* that, on the night of 22–23 May 1844, the Báb (a title meaning 'Gate') announced that He was the Bearer of a Divine Revelation destined not only to transform Islam but to set a new direction for the spiritual life of humankind.

During the decade that followed, mounting opposition from both clergy and state brought about the martyrdom of the Báb, the massacre of His leading disciples and of several thousands of His followers, and the virtual extinction of the religious system that He had founded. Out of

---

*   Mullá Ḥusayn-i-Bushrú'í.

these harrowing years, however, emerged a successor movement, the Bahá'í Faith, that has since spread throughout
the planet and established its claim to represent a new and
independent world religion.

It is to Bahá'u'lláh (Mírzá Ḥusayn-'Alí, 1817–1892),
that the worldwide Bahá'í community looks as the source of
its spiritual and social teachings, the authority for the laws
and institutions that shape its life, and the vision of unity
that has today made it one of the most geographically widespread and ethnically diverse of organized bodies of people
on the planet. It is from Bahá'u'lláh that the Faith derives
its name and toward Whose resting place in the Holy Land
that the millions of Bahá'ís around the world daily direct
their thoughts when they turn to God in prayer.

These circumstances in no way diminish, however, the
fact that the new Faith was born amid the bloody and terrible magnificence surrounding the Báb's brief mission, nor
that the inspiration for its worldwide spread has been the
spirit of self-sacrifice that Bahá'ís find in His life and the
lives of the heroic band that followed Him. Prayers revealed
by the Báb and passages from His voluminous writings are
part of the devotional life of Bahá'ís everywhere. The events
of His mission are commemorated as annual holy days in
tens of thousands of local Bahá'í communities.* On the
slopes of Mount Carmel, the golden-domed Shrine where
His mortal remains are buried dominates the great complex
of monumental buildings and gardens constituting the
administrative center of the Faith's international activities.

---

* The anniversary of the birth of the Báb is observed on the first day following
  the occurrence of the eighth new moon after Naw-Rúz, as determined in
  advance by astronomical tables using Tehran as the point of reference. The
  birthday moves year to year, within the months of Mashíyyat, 'Ilm, and
  Qudrat of the Badí' calendar, or from mid-October to mid-November
  according to the Gregorian calendar. The Declaration of the Báb is marked
  on 8 'Aẓamat; the Martyrdom of the Báb on 17 Raḥmat.

In contemporary public awareness of the Bahá'í community and its activities, however, the life and person of Bahá'u'lláh have largely overshadowed those of the Báb. In a sense, it is natural that this should be the case, given the primary role of Bahá'u'lláh as the fulfillment of the Báb's promises and the Architect of the Faith's achievements. To some extent, however, this circumstance also reflects the painfully slow emergence of the new religion from obscurity onto the stage of history. In a perceptive comment on the subject, the British historian Arnold Toynbee compared the level of appreciation of the Bahá'í Faith in most Western lands with the similarly limited impression that the mission of Jesus Christ had succeeded in making on the educated class in the Roman Empire some 300 years after His death.[*] Since most of the public activity of the Bahá'í community over the past several decades has focused on the demanding task of presenting Bahá'u'lláh's message, and elaborating the implications of its social teachings for the life of society, the Faith's nineteenth-century Persian origins have tended to become temporarily eclipsed in the public mind.

Indeed, Bahá'ís, too, are challenged by the implications of the extraordinary idea that our age has witnessed the appearance of two almost contemporaneous Messengers of God. Bahá'u'lláh describes the phenomenon as one of the distinguishing characteristics of the new religion and as a mystery central to the plan of God for the unification of humankind and the establishment of a global civilization.[†]

Fundamental to the Bahá'í conception of the evolution of civilization is an analogy to be found in the writings of both the Báb and Bahá'u'lláh. It draws a parallel between the

---

[*] Arnold Toynbee, *A Study of History*, vol. 8 (London: Oxford, 1954), p. 117.

[†] Shoghi Effendi, *The World Order of Bahá'u'lláh: Selected Letters*, 2nd rev. ed. (Wilmette, Ill: Bahá'í Publishing Trust, 1974), pp. 123–124.

process by which the human race has gradually been civilized and that whereby each one of its individual members passes through the successive stages of infancy, childhood, and adolescence to adulthood. The idea throws a measure of light on the relationship which Bahá'ís see between the missions of the two Founders of their religion.

Both the Báb and Bahá'u'lláh – the former implicitly and the latter explicitly – describe the human race as standing now on the brink of its collective maturity. Apart from the Báb's role as a Messenger of God, His advent marks the fruition of the process of the refining of human nature which thousands of years of Divine revelation have cultivated. It can be viewed, in that sense, as the gateway through which humankind must pass as it takes up the responsibilities of maturity. Its brevity itself seems symbolic of the relative suddenness of the transition.*

At the individual level, no sooner does one cross the critical threshold of maturity in his or her development than the challenges and opportunities of adulthood beckon. The emerging potentialities of human life must now find expression through the long years of responsibility and achievement: they must become actualized through marriage, a profession and family, and service to society. In the collective life of humanity, it is the mission of Bahá'u'lláh, the universal Messenger of God anticipated in the scriptures of all the world's religions, to size up our age's emerging consciousness of universal brotherhood and to generate the unity of thought and of collective action that will be the distinguishing characteristic of the maturity of the race. This alone can lay the foundations of global civilization.

❧

---

*   I owe this interesting suggestion to Dr Hossain Danesh.

Even as late as the end of the nineteenth century, however, it was the Báb who figured as the central Personality of the new religion among most of those Westerners who had become aware of its existence. Writing in the American periodical *Forum* in 1925, the French literary critic Jules Bois remembered the extraordinary impact which the story of the Báb continued to have on educated opinion in Europe as the nineteenth century closed:

> All Europe was stirred to pity and indignation ... Among the littérateurs of my generation, in the Paris of 1890, the martyrdom of the Báb was still as fresh a topic as had been the first news of His death [in 1850]. We wrote poems about Him. Sarah Bernhardt entreated Catulle Mendès for a play on the theme of this historic tragedy.*

Writers as diverse as Joseph Arthur de Gobineau, Edward Granville Browne, Ernest Renan, Aleksandr Tumanskiy, A. L. M. Nicolas, Viktor Rosen, Clément Huart, George Curzon, Matthew Arnold, and Leo Tolstoy were affected by the spiritual drama that had unfolded in Persia during the middle years of the nineteenth century. Not until the early part of our own century did the name the 'Bahá'í Cause', which the new religion had already adopted for itself as early as the 1860s, replace the designation of 'Bábí movement' in general usage in the West.†

That this should have been the case was no doubt a reflection of the degree to which the brief but incandescent life of

---

* Shoghi Effendi, *God Passes By* (1944; reprint, Wilmette, IL: Bahá'í Publishing Trust, 1974), p. 56 and *The Bahá'í World*, vol. IX (1940–1944) (1945; reprint, Wilmette, Ill: Bahá'í Publishing Trust, 1981), p. 588.

† Persistent use of the term 'Bábí' in Iranian Muslim attacks on the Bahá'í Faith over the years has tended to be a reflection of the spirit of animosity incited by its original nineteenth-century clerical opponents.

the Báb seemed to catch up and embody cultural ideals that had dominated European thought during the first half of the nineteenth century, and which exercised a powerful influence on the Western imagination for many decades thereafter. The concept commonly used to describe the course of Europe's cultural and intellectual development during the first five or six decades of the nineteenth century is Romanticism. By the century's beginning, European thought had begun to look beyond its preoccupation with the arid rationalism and mechanistic certainties of the Enlightenment toward an exploration of other dimensions of existence: the aesthetic, the emotional, the intuitive, the mystical, the 'natural', the 'irrational'. Literature, philosophy, history, music, and art all responded strongly and gradually exerted a sympathetic influence on the popular mind.

In England, where the tendency was already gathering force as the century opened, one effect was to produce perhaps the most spectacular outpouring of lyrical poetry that the language has ever known. Over the next two to three decades these early insights were to find powerful echoes throughout Western Europe. A new order of things, a whole new world, lay within reach, if man would only dare what was needed. Liberated by the intellectual upheaval of the preceding decades, poets, artists and musicians conceived of themselves as the voice of immense creative capacities latent in human consciousness and seeking expression; as 'prophets' shaping a new conception of human nature and human society. With the validity of traditional religion now shrouded in doubt, mythical figures and events from the classical past were summoned up to serve as vehicles for this heroic Ideal:

To suffer woes which Hope thinks infinite;
To forgive wrongs darker than Death or Night;

To defy Power which seems Omnipotent;
To love, and bear; to hope, till Hope creates
From its own wreck the thing it contemplates . . .
This alone is Life, Joy, Empire and Victory.*

The same longings had awakened in America in the decades immediately preceding the Civil War and were to leave an indelible imprint on public consciousness. All of the transcendentalists became deeply attracted by the mystical literature of the Orient: the Bhagavad Gita, the Ramayana, and the Upanishads, as well as the works of the major Islamic poets, Rumí, Hafez, and Sa'adí. The effect can be appreciated in such influential writings of Emerson as the Divinity School Address:

> I look for the hour when that supreme Beauty which ravished the souls of those eastern Men, and chiefly those of the Hebrews, and through their lips spoke oracles to all time, shall speak in the West also . . . I look for the new Teacher that shall follow so far those shining laws that He shall see them come full circle; . . . shall see the world to be the mirror of the soul; shall see the identity of the law of gravitation with purity of heart; and shall show . . . that Duty is one thing with Science, with Beauty, and with Joy.†

As the century advanced, the early Romantic optimism found itself increasingly mired in the successive disappointments and defeats of the revolutionary fervor it had helped arouse. Under the pressure of scientific and technological

---

* Percy Bysshe Shelley, *Prometheus Unbound*, bk. 4, ll. 569–578.
† Ralph Waldo Emerson, 'The Divinity School Address', *Selections from Ralph Waldo Emerson*, S. E. Wricher, ed. (Boston: Houghton Mifflin, 1960), pp. 115–116.

change, the culture of philosophical materialism to which enlightenment speculation had originally given rise gradually consolidated itself. The wars and revolutionary upheavals of the middle years of the century contributed further to a mood of 'realism', a recognition that great ideals must somehow be reconciled with the obdurate circumstances of human nature.

Even in the relatively sober atmosphere of Victorian public discourse, however, Romantic yearnings retained a potent influence in Western consciousness. They produced a susceptibility to spiritual impulses which, while different from that which had characterized the opening decades of the century, now affected a broad public. If the revolutionary figure of Prometheus no longer spoke to English perceptions of the age, the Arthurian legend caught up the popular hope, blending youthful idealism with the insights of maturity, and capturing the imagination of millions precisely on that account:

> The old order changeth, yielding place to new,
> And God fulfils himself in many ways,
> Lest one good custom should corrupt the world.*

It is hardly surprising that, on minds formed in this cultural milieu, the figure of the Báb should exert a compelling fascination, as Westerners became acquainted with His story in the latter years of the century. Particularly appealing was the purity of His life, an unshadowed nobility of character that had won the hearts of many among His fellow countrymen who had come as doubters or even enemies and stayed to lay down their lives in His cause. Words which the Báb addressed to the first group of His disciples suggest the

---

* Alfred Lord Tennyson, *Idylls of the King: The Passing of Arthur*, ll. 408–410.

nature of the moral standards He held up as goals for those who responded to His call:

> Purge your hearts of worldly desires, and let angelic virtues be your adorning. . . . The days when idle worship was deemed sufficient are ended. The time is come when naught but the purest motive, supported by deeds of stainless purity, can ascend to the throne of the Most High and be acceptable unto Him. . . . Beseech the Lord your God to grant that no earthly entanglements, no worldly affections, no ephemeral pursuits, may tarnish the purity, or embitter the sweetness, of that grace which flows through you.[*]

Purity of heart was coupled with a courage and willingness for self-sacrifice that Western observers found deeply inspiring. The commentaries of Ernest Renan and others drew the inescapable parallel with the life of Jesus Christ. As the extraordinary drama of His final moments convincingly demonstrated,[†] the Báb could have at any moment saved

---

[*] Muḥammad-i-Zarandí (Nabíl-i-A'ẓam), *The Dawn-Breakers: Nabíl's Narrative of the Early Days of the Baháʼí Revelation*, translated from the Persian by Shoghi Effendi (1932; reprint, Wilmette, IL: Baháʼí Publishing Trust, 1974), p. 93.

[†] The Báb, together with a young follower, was suspended by ropes from a courtyard wall in the citadel in Tabríz, and an Armenian Christian regiment, whose commander had expressed great uneasiness about the assignment, was ordered to open fire on the prisoners. When the smoke from the 750 rifles had cleared, near pandemonium broke out among the crowd of spectators thronging roofs and walls. The Báb's companion was standing uninjured at the foot of the wall, and the Báb Himself had disappeared from view. The entire volley had done no more than sever the ropes. The Báb had returned to the room in which He had been held, in order to complete instructions to His amanuensis, which had been interrupted by His jailers.

The Armenian regiment immediately left the citadel, refusing any further participation. It would have taken only a gesture of encouragement from the Báb for the crowd, now in a state of intense excitement aroused by what they regarded as 'a miracle', to have delivered Him from His captors.

Himself and achieved mastery over those who persecuted
Him by taking advantage of the folly of His adversaries and
the superstition of the general populace. He scorned to do
so, and accepted death at the hands of His enemies only
when satisfied that His mission had been completed in its
entirety and in conformity with the Will of God. His followers, who had divested themselves of all earthly attachments
and advantages, were barbarously massacred by adversaries
who had sworn on the Qur'án to spare their lives and their
honor, and who shamefully abused their wives and children
after their deaths. Renan writes:

> Des milliers de martyrs sont accourus pour lui avec
> l'allégresse au devant de la mort. Un jour sans pareil
> peut-être dans l'histoire du monde fut celui de la grande
> boucherie qui se fit des Bábís, à Téhéran. 'On vit ce
> jour-là dans les rues et les bazars de Téhéran,' dit un
> narrateur qui a tout su d'original, 'un spectacle que la
> population semble devoir n'oublier jamais. . . . Enfants
> et femmes s'avançaient en chantant un verset qui dit:
> En vérité nous venons de Dieu et nous retournons à
> Lui.'*

When He did not take advantage of this opening, the authorities eventually
recovered their composure and summoned a regiment of Muslim soldiers
who carried out the planned execution.

 Though dramatic, the incident was not an isolated event in the Báb's
ministry. Four years earlier, the wealthy and powerful Governor of Iṣfáhán,
Manúchir Khán, who was the Báb's host and warm admirer, had offered
to march on the capital with his army and induce Persia's feeble ruler,
Muḥammad Sháh, to meet the Báb and listen to His message. The offer was
courteously declined, and Manúchir Khán's subsequent death led directly
to the Báb's arrest, imprisonment, and execution.

* Ernest Renan, *Les Apôtres*, translated from the French by William G.
Hutchison (London: Watts & Co., 1905), p. 134. 'For his sake, thousands
of martyrs flocked to their death. A day unparalleled perhaps in the world's
history was that of the great massacre of the Bábís at Teheran. "On that
day was to be seen in the streets and bazaars of Teheran," says a narrator,

Purity of heart and moral courage were matched by an idealism with which most Western observers could also readily identify. By the nineteenth century, the Persia to which the Báb addressed Himself and which had once been one of the world's great civilizations, had sunk to an object of despair and contempt among foreign visitors. A population ignorant, apathetic, and superstitious in the extreme was the prey of a profoundly corrupt Muslim clergy and the brutal regime of the Qájár shahs. Shí'ih Islam had, for the most part, degenerated into a mass of superstitions and mindless legalisms. Security of life and property depended entirely on the whims of those in authority.

Such was the society that the Báb summoned to reflection and self-discipline. A new age had dawned; God demanded purity of heart rather than religious formulae, an inner condition that must be matched by cleanliness in all aspects of daily life; truth was a goal to be won not by blind imitation but by personal effort, prayer, meditation, and detachment from the appetites. The nature of the accounts which Western writers like Gobineau, Browne, and Nicolas were later to hear from surviving followers of the Báb can be appreciated from the words in which Mullá Ḥusayn-i-Bushrú'í described the effect on him of his first meeting with the Báb:

> I felt possessed of such courage and power that were the world, all its peoples and its potentates, to rise against me, I would, alone and undaunted, withstand their onslaught. The universe seemed but a handful of dust

who has first-hand knowledge, "a spectacle which it does not seem that the populations can ever forget . . .Women and children advanced, singing a verse, which says: 'In truth we come from God, and unto him we return'." The narrator referred to is J. A. de Gobineau, 3d ed., *Les Religions et les Philosophies dans l'Asie Centrale* (Paris: Ernest Leroux, 1900), p. 304 et seq.

in my grasp. I seemed to be the Voice of Gabriel personified, calling unto all mankind: 'Awake, for, lo! the
morning Light has broken.'[*]

European observers, visiting the country long after the Báb's
martyrdom, were struck by the moral distinction achieved
by Persia's Bahá'í community. Explaining to Western readers
the success of Bahá'í teaching activities among the Persian
population, in contrast to the ineffectual efforts of Christian missionaries, E. G. Browne said:

> To the Western observer, however, it is the complete sin-
> cerity of the Bábís [sic], their fearless disregard of death
> and torture undergone for the sake of their religion,
> their certain conviction as to the truth of their faith,
> their generally admirable conduct towards mankind
> and especially towards their fellow-believers, which
> constitutes their strongest claim on his attention.[†]

The figure of the Báb appealed strongly also to aesthetic
sensibilities which Romanticism had awakened. Apart from
those of His countrymen whose positions were threatened by
His mission, surviving accounts by all who met Him agree in
their description of the extraordinary beauty of His person
and of His physical movements. His voice, particularly when
chanting the tablets and prayers He revealed, possessed a
sweetness that captivated the heart. Even His clothing and
the furnishings of His simple house were marked by a degree
of refinement that seemed to reflect the inner spiritual beauty
that so powerfully attracted His visitors.

---

[*] *The Dawn-Breakers*, p. 65.
[†] E. G. Browne, introduction to Myron H. Phelps, *Life and Teachings of Abbas Effendi*, 2nd rev. ed. (New York; London: G. P. Putnam's Sons: The Knickerbocker Press, 1912), p. xvi.

Particular reference must be made to the originality of the Báb's thought and the manner in which He chose to express it. Throughout all the vicissitudes of the nineteenth century, the European mind had continued to cling to the ideal of the 'man of destiny' who, through the sheer creative force of his untrammeled genius, could set a new course in human affairs. At the beginning of the century, Napoleon Bonaparte had seemed to represent such a phenomenon, and not even the disillusionment that had followed his betrayal of the ideal had discouraged the powerful current of individualism that was one of the Romantic movement's principal legacies to the century and, indeed, to our own.

Out of the Báb's writings emerges a sweeping new approach to religious truth. Its sheer boldness was one of the principal reasons for the violence of the opposition that His work aroused among the obscurantist Muslim clergy who dominated all serious discourse in nineteenth-century Persia. These challenging concepts were matched by the highly innovative character of the language in which they were communicated.

In its literary form, Arabic possesses an almost hypnotic beauty – a beauty which, in the language of the Qur'án, attains levels of the sublime which Muslims of all ages have regarded as beyond imitation by mortal man. For all Muslims, regardless of their sect, culture, or nation, Arabic is the language of Revelation par excellence. The proof of the Divine origin of the Qur'án lay not chiefly in its character as literature, but in the power its verses possessed to change human behavior and attitudes. Although, like Jesus and Muḥammad before Him, the Báb had little formal schooling, He used both Arabic and His native Persian, alternately, as the themes of His discourse required.

To His hearers, the most dramatic sign of the Báb's

spiritual authority was that, for the first time in more than twelve centuries, human ears were privileged to hear again the inimitable accents of Revelation. Indeed, in one important respect, the Qur'án was far surpassed. Tablets, meditations, and prayers of thrilling power flowed effortlessly from the lips of the Báb. In one extraordinary period of two days, His writings exceeded in quantity the entire text of the Qur'án, which represented the fruit of 23 years of Muḥammad's prophetic output. No one among His ecclesiastical opponents ventured to take up His public challenge: 'Verily We have made the revelation of verses to be a testimony for Our message to you.' [i.e., In the Qur'án God had explicitly established the 'miracle' of the Book's power as His sole proof.] 'Can ye produce a single letter to match these verses? Bring forth, then, your proofs. . . .'*

Moreover, despite His ability to use traditional Arabic forms when He chose to do so, the Báb showed no hesitancy in abandoning these conventions as the requirements of His message dictated. He resorted freely to neologisms, new grammatical constructions, and other variants on accepted speech whenever He found existing terms inadequate vehicles for the revolutionary new conception of spiritual reality He vigorously advanced. Rebuked by learned Shí'ih mujtahids at His trial in Tabríz (1848) for violations of the rules of grammar, the Báb reminded those who followed Him that the Word of God is the Creator of language as of all other things, shaping it according to His purpose.† Through the power of His Word, God says 'BE', and it is.

The principle is as old as prophetic religion; – is indeed, central to it:

---

* The Báb, *Selections from the Writings of the Báb* (Haifa: Bahá'í World Centre, 1976), p. 43.
† *The Dawn-Breakers*, pp. 321–322.

In the beginning was the Word, and the Word was with
God, and the Word was God. . . .
All things were made by him; and without him was not
any thing made that was made. . . .
He was in the world, and the world was made by him,
and the world knew him not.*

The implications for humanity's response to the Messenger
of God at His advent is touched on in a passage of one of
Bahá'u'lláh's major works, The Four Valleys. Quoting the
Persian poet Rumi, He says:

The story is told of a mystic knower, who went on a
journey with a learned grammarian as his companion.
They came to the shore of the Sea of Grandeur. The
knower straightway flung himself into the waves, but
the grammarian stood lost in his reasonings, which
were as words that are written on water. The knower
called out to him, 'Why dost thou not follow?' The
grammarian answered, 'O Brother, I dare not advance.
I must needs go back again.' Then the knower cried,
'Forget what thou didst read in the books of [rhetoric
and grammar], and cross the water.'
  The death of self is needed here, not rhetoric:
  Be nothing, then, and walk upon the waves.†

For the young seminarians who most eagerly responded to
Him, the originality of the Báb's language, far from creating an obstacle to their appreciation of His message, itself
represented another compelling sign of the Divine mission

*   John 1:1–10, Authorized (King James) Version.
†   Bahá'u'lláh, The Seven Valleys and the Four Valleys (1978; reprint Wilmette,
    Ill: Bahá'í Publishing Trust, 1984), pp. 51–52.

He claimed. It challenged them to break out of familiar patterns of perception, to stretch their intellectual faculties, to discover in this new Revelation a true freedom of the spirit. However baffling some of the Báb's writings were to prove for His later European admirers, the latter also perceived Him to be a unique figure, one who had found within His own soul the vision of a transcendent new reality and who had acted unhesitatingly on the imperative it represented. Most of their commentaries tended to reflect the Victorian era's dualistic frame of mind and were presented as scientifically motivated observations of what their authors considered to be an important religious and cultural phenomenon. In the introduction to his translation of *A Traveller's Narrative*, for example, the Cambridge scholar Edward Granville Browne took pains to justify the unusual degree of attention he had devoted to the Bábí movement in his research work:

> . . . here he [the student of religion] may contemplate such personalities as by lapse of time pass into heroes and demi-gods still unobscured by myth and fable; he may examine by the light of concurrent and independent testimony one of those strange outbursts of enthusiasm, faith, fervent devotion, and indomitable heroism – or fanaticism, if you will – which we are accustomed to associate with the earlier history of the human race; he may witness, in a word, the birth of a faith which may not impossibly win a place amidst the great religions of the world.*

The electrifying effect that the phenomenon exerted,

---

* E. G. Browne, Introduction to *A Traveller's Narrative: Written to Illustrate the Episode of the Báb*, by 'Abdu'l-Bahá. Trans. E. G. Browne (New York: Bahá'í Publishing Committee, 1930), p. viii.

however – even on a cautious and scientifically trained European intellect and after the passage of several decades – can be appreciated from Browne's concluding remarks in a major article in *Religious Systems of the World*, published in 1892, the year of Bahá'u'lláh's passing:

> I trust that I have told you enough to make it clear that the objects at which this religion aims are neither trivial nor unworthy of the noble self-devotion and heroism of the Founder and his followers. It is the lives and deaths of these, their hope which knows no despair, their love which knows no cooling, their steadfastness which knows no wavering, which stamp this wonderful movement with a character entirely its own. . . .
>
> It is not a small or easy thing to endure what these have endured, and surely what they deemed worth life itself is worth trying to understand. I say nothing of the mighty influence which, as I believe, the Bábí faith will exert in the future, nor of the new life it may perchance breathe into a dead people; for, whether it succeed or fail, the splendid heroism of the Bábí martyrs is a thing eternal and indestructible.[*]

So powerful was this impression that most Western observers tended to lose sight of the Báb's purpose through fascination with His life and person. Browne himself, whose research made him pre-eminent among the second generation of European authorities on the Bábí movement, largely failed to grasp the role the Báb's mission played in preparing the way for the work of Bahá'u'lláh or, indeed, the way in

---

[*]   E. G. Browne, 'Bábíism', *Religious Systems of the World*, 3rd edition (London: Swan Sonnenschein & Co. and New York: MacMillan & Co., 1892), pp. 352–353.

which the achievements of the latter represented the Báb's eventual triumph and vindication.* The French writer A. L. M. Nicolas was much more fortunate, in part simply because he lived long enough to benefit from a greater historical perspective. Initially antagonistic toward what he saw as Bahá'u'lláh's 'supplanting' of the Báb, he came finally to appreciate the Bahá'í view that the Báb was one of two successive Manifestations of God whose joint mission is the unification and pacification of the planet.†

∾

This brief historical framework will be of assistance in understanding the thrust of the Báb's teachings. In one sense, His message is abundantly clear. As He repeatedly emphasized, the purpose of His mission and the object of all His endeavours was the proclamation of the imminent advent of 'Him Whom God will make manifest', that universal Manifestation of God anticipated in religious scriptures throughout the ages of human history. Indeed, all of the laws revealed by the Báb were intended simply to prepare His followers to recognize and serve the Promised One at His advent:

We have planted the Garden of the Bayán [i.e., His Revelation] in the name of Him Whom God will make

---

* Browne's objectivity appears to have been clouded, as well, by his hope that the Bábís would focus their energies on the political reform of Persia itself. Criticizing what he saw as Bahá'u'lláh's diversion of Bahá'í energies from domestic politics to the cause of world unity, he complained that '. . . just now it is men who love their country above all else that Persia needs'. English introduction to the *Nuqtatu'l-Káf*, cited in H. M. Balyuzi, *Edward Granville Browne and the Bahá'í Faith* (London: George Ronald, 1970), p. 88.

† *The Bahá'í World*, vol. IX (1940–44) (Wilmette, IL: Bahá'í Publishing Trust, 1945), pp. 584–585.

manifest, and have granted you permission to live therein until the time of His manifestation. . . .*

The Báb's mission was to prepare humanity for the coming of an age of transformation beyond anything the generation that heard Him would be able to understand. Their duty was to purify their hearts so that they could recognize the One for Whom the whole world was waiting and serve the establishment of the Kingdom of God. The Báb was thus the 'Door' through which this long-awaited universal theophany would appear.

> At the time of the appearance of Him Whom God will make manifest the most distinguished among the learned and the lowliest of men shall both be judged alike. How often the most insignificant of men have acknowledged the truth, while the most learned have remained wrapt in veils.†

Significantly, the initial references to the Promised Deliverer appear in the Báb's first major work, the Qayyúmu'l-Asmá', passages of which were revealed by Him on the night of the declaration of His mission. The entire work is ostensibly a collection of commentaries on the Súrih of Joseph in the Qur'án, which the Báb interprets as foreshadowing the coming of the Divine 'Joseph', that 'Remnant of God' Who will fulfill the promises of the Qur'án and of all the other scriptures of the past. More than any other work, the Qayyúmu'l-Asmá' vindicated for Bábís the prophetic claims of its Author and served, throughout the early part of the Báb's ministry, as the Qur'án or the Bible of His community.

---

*   *Selections from the Writings of the Báb*, p. 135.
†   ibid. p. 91.

O peoples of the East and the West! Be ye fearful of God concerning the Cause of the true Joseph and barter Him not for a paltry price established by yourselves, or for a trifle of your earthly possessions, that ye may, in very truth, be praised by Him as those who are reckoned among the pious who stand nigh unto this Gate.*

In 1848, only two years before His martyrdom, the Báb revealed the Bayán, the book which was to serve as the principal repository of his laws and the fullest expression of His theological doctrines. Essentially the book is an extended tribute to the coming Promised One, now invariably termed 'Him Whom God will make manifest'. The latter designation occurs some 300 times in the book, appearing in virtually every one of its chapters, regardless of their ostensible subject. The Bayán and all it contains depend upon His Will; the whole of the Bayán contains in fact 'nought but His mention'; the Bayán is 'a humble gift' from its Author to Him Whom God will make manifest; to attain His Presence is to attain the Presence of God. He is 'the Sun of Truth', 'the Advent of Truth', 'the Point of Truth', 'the Tree of Truth':†

I swear by the most holy Essence of God – exalted and glorified be He – that in the Day of the appearance of Him Whom God shall make manifest a thousand perusals of the Bayán cannot equal the perusal of a single verse to be revealed by Him Whom God shall make manifest.‡

---

* ibid. p. 49.
† Persian Bayán, unpublished manuscript. References to units and chapters 7.1; 5.7; 4.1; and 7.11.
‡ *Selections from the Writings of the Báb*, p. 104.

Some of the most powerful references to the subject are contained in Tablets which the Báb addressed directly to Him Whom God would soon make manifest:

> Out of utter nothingness, O great and omnipotent Master, Thou hast, through the celestial potency of Thy might, brought me forth and raised me up to proclaim this Revelation. I have made none other but Thee my trust; I have clung to no will but Thy Will. Thou art, in truth, the All-Sufficing and behind Thee standeth the true God, He Who overshadoweth all things.*

Apart from this central theme, the Báb's writings present a daunting problem for even those Western scholars familiar with Persian and Arabic. To a considerable degree, this is due to the fact that the works often address minute matters of Shí'ih Islamic theology which were of consuming importance to His listeners, whose minds had been entirely formed in this narrow intellectual world and who could conceive of no other. The study of the organizing spiritual principles within these writings will doubtless occupy generations of doctoral candidates as the Bahá'í community continues to expand and its influence in the life of society consolidates. For the Bábís, who received the writings at first hand, a great deal of their significance lay in their demonstration of the Báb's effortless mastery of the most abstruse theological issues, issues to which His ecclesiastical opponents had devoted years of painstaking study and dispute. The effect was to dissolve for the Báb's followers the intellectual foundations on which the prevailing Islamic theological system rested.

A feature of the Báb's writings which is relatively accessible is the laws they contain. The Báb revealed what is, at

---

* ibid. p. 59.

first sight, the essential elements of a complete system of laws dealing with issues of both daily life and social organization. The question that comes immediately to the mind of any Western reader with even a cursory familiarity with Bábí history is the difficulty of reconciling this body of law which, however diffuse, might well have prevailed for several centuries, with the Báb's reiterated anticipation that 'He Whom God will make manifest' would shortly appear and lay the foundations of the Kingdom of God. While no one knew the hour of His coming, the Báb assured several of His followers that they would live to see and serve Him. Cryptic allusions to 'the year nine' and 'the year nineteen' heightened the anticipation within the Bábí community. No one could falsely claim to be 'He Whom God will make manifest', the Báb asserted, and succeed in such a claim.

It is elsewhere that we must look for the immediate significance of the laws of the Bayán. The practice of Islam, particularly in its Shí'ih form, had become a matter of adherence to minutely detailed ordinances and prescriptions, endlessly elaborated by generations of mujtahids, and rigidly enforced. The sharí'a, or system of canon law, was, in effect, the embodiment of the clergy's authority over not only the mass of the population but even the monarchy itself. It contained all that mankind needed or could use. The mouth of God was closed until the Day of Judgment when the heavens would be cleft asunder, the mountains would dissolve, the seas would boil, trumpet blasts would rouse the dead from their graves, and God would 'come down' surrounded by angels 'rank on rank'.

For those who recognized the Báb, the legal provisions of the Bayán shattered the clergy's institutional authority at one blow by making the entire sharí'a structure irrelevant.*

---

*   The challenge came into sharp focus for the Báb's leading followers at a

God had spoken anew. Challenged by a superannuated religious establishment which claimed to act in the name of the Prophet, the Báb vindicated His claim by exercising, in their fullness, the authority and powers that Islam reserved to the Prophets. More than any other act of His mission, it was this boldness that cost Him His life, but the effect was to liberate the minds and hearts of His followers as no other influence could have done. That so many laws of the Bayán should shortly be superseded or significantly altered by those laid down by Bahá'u'lláh in the Kitáb-i-Aqdas* was, in the perspective of history and in the eyes of the mass of the Bábís who were to accept the new Revelation, of little significance once the Báb's purpose had been accomplished.

In this connection, it is interesting to note the way in which the Báb dealt with issues that had no part in His mission, but which, if not addressed, could have become serious obstacles to His work because they were so deeply and firmly imbedded in Muslim religious consciousness. The concept of *jihád* or 'holy war', for example, is a commandment laid down in the Qur'an as obligatory for all able-bodied male Muslims and one whose practice has figured prominently in Islamic societies throughout the ages. In the Qayyúmu'l-Asmá', the Báb is at pains to include a form of jihád as one of the prerogatives of the station which He claims for Himself. He made any engagement in jihád, however, entirely dependent on His own approval, an approval which He declined to give. Subsequently, the Bayán, although representing the formal promulgation of

---

conference held at the small hamlet of Badasht in 1848. Interestingly, the figure who took the lead in bringing about a realization of the magnitude of the spiritual and intellectual changes set in motion by the Báb was a woman, the gifted poetess Ṭáhirih, who was also later to suffer martyrdom for her beliefs.

* 'The Most Holy Book', Bahá'u'lláh's charter for a new world civilization, written in Arabic in 1873.

the laws of the new Dispensation, makes only passing reference to a subject which had so long seemed fundamental to the exercise of God's Will. In ranging across Persia to proclaim the new Revelation, therefore, the Báb's followers felt free to defend themselves when attacked, but their new beliefs did not include the old Islamic mandate to wage war on others for purposes of conversion.*

In the perspective of history, it is obvious that the intent of these rigid and exacting laws was to produce a spiritual mobilization, and in this they brilliantly succeeded. Foreseeing clearly where the course on which he was embarked would lead, the Báb prepared His followers, through a severe regimen of prayer, meditation, self-discipline, and solidarity of community life, to meet the inevitable consequences of their commitment to His mission.

The prescriptions in the Bayán extend, however, far beyond those immediate purposes. Consequently, when Bahá'u'lláh took up the task of establishing the moral and spiritual foundations of the new Dispensation, He built directly on the work of the Báb. The Kitáb-i-Aqdas, the 'Mother Book' of the Bahá'í era, while not presented in the form of a systematic code, brings together for Bahá'ís the principal laws of their Faith. Guidance that relates to individual conduct or social practice is set in the framework of passages which summon the reader to a challenging new conception of human nature and purpose. A nineteenth-century Russian scholar who made one of the early attempts to translate the book compared Bahá'u'lláh's pen writing the Aqdas to a bird, now soaring on the summits of heaven, now descending to touch the homeliest questions of everyday need.

---

* In the Kitáb-i-Aqdas Bahá'u'lláh formally abolishes holy war as a feature of religious life. See William S. Hatcher and J. Douglas Martin, *The Bahá'í Faith: The Emerging Global Religion* (San Francisco: Harper & Row, 1985), pp. 13–14.

The connection with the writings of the Báb is readily apparent to anyone who examines the provisions of the Aqdas. Those laws of the Bayán which have no relevance to the coming age are abrogated. Other prescriptions are reformulated, usually through liberalizing their requirements and broadening their applications. Still other provisions of the Bayán are retained virtually in their original form. An obvious example of the latter is Bahá'u'lláh's adoption of the Báb's calendar, which consists of nineteen months of nineteen days each, with provision for an 'intercalary' period of four or five days devoted to social gatherings, acts of charity, and the exchange of gifts with friends and family.

❧

Apart from the specific laws of the Bayán, the Báb's writings also contain the seeds of new spiritual perspectives and concepts which were to animate the worldwide Bahá'í enterprise. Beginning from the belief universally accepted by Muslims that God is one and transcendent, the Báb cuts sharply through the welter of conflicting doctrines and mystical speculations that had accumulated over more than twelve centuries of Islamic history. God is not only One and Single; He is utterly unknowable to humankind and will forever remain so. There is no direct connection between the Creator of all things and His creation.

The only avenue of approach to the Divine Reality behind existence is through the succession of Messengers Whom He sends. God 'manifests' Himself to humanity in this fashion, and it is in the Person of His Manifestation that human consciousness can become aware of both the Divine Will and the Divine attributes. What the scriptures have described as 'meeting God', 'knowing God', 'worshiping God', 'serving God', refers to the response of the soul when it recognizes the new Revelation. The advent of the Messenger of God is itself 'the Day of Judgment'. The Báb thus denies the validity of Ṣúfí belief in the possibility of the individual's mystical merging with the Divine Being through meditation and esoteric practices:

> Deceive not your own selves that you are being virtuous for the sake of God when you are not. For should ye truly do your works for God, ye would be performing them for Him Whom God shall make manifest and would be magnifying His Name. . . . Ponder awhile that ye may not be shut out as by a veil from Him Who is the Dayspring of Revelation.*

Going far beyond the orthodox Islamic conception of a 'succession' of the Prophets that terminates with the mission of Muḥammad, the Báb also declares the Revelation of God to be a recurring and never-ending phenomenon whose purpose is the gradual training and development of humankind. As human consciousness recognizes and responds to each Divine Messenger, the spiritual, moral, and intellectual capacities latent in it steadily develop, thus preparing the way for recognition of God's next Manifestation.

The Manifestations of God – including Abraham, Moses, Jesus, and Muḥammad – are one in essence, although their physical persons differ, as do those aspects of their teachings that relate to an ever evolving human society. Each can be said to have two 'stations': the human and the Divine. Each brings two proofs of His mission: His own Person and the truths He teaches. Either of these testimonies is sufficient for any sincerely inquiring soul; the issue is purity

---

* *Selections from the Writings of the Báb*, p. 86.

of intention, and this human quality is particularly valued in the Báb's writings. Through unity of faith, reason and behavior, each person can, with the confirmations of God, reach that stage of development where one seeks for others the same things that one seeks for oneself.

Those who sincerely believe in the Messenger whose faith they follow are prepared by it to recognize the next Revelation from the one Divine Source. They thus become instruments through which the Word of God continues to realize its purpose in the life of humankind. This is the real meaning of the references in past religions to 'resurrection'. 'Heaven' and 'hell', similarly, are not places but conditions of the soul. An individual 'enters' paradise in this world when he recognizes God's Revelation and begins the process of perfecting his nature, a process that has no end, since the soul itself is immortal. In the same way, the punishments of God are inherent in a denial of His Revelation and disobedience to laws whose operation no one can escape.

Many of these concepts in the Báb's writing can appeal to various references or at least intimations in the scriptures of earlier religions. It will be obvious from what has been said, however, that the Báb places them in an entirely new context and draws from them implications very different from those which they bore in any previous religious system.

The Báb described His teachings as opening the 'sealed wine' referred to in both the Qur'án and New Testament. The 'Day of God' does not envision the end of the world, but its perennial renewal. The earth will continue to exist, as will the human race, whose potentialities will progressively unfold in response to the successive impulses of the Divine. All people are equal in the sight of God, and the race has now advanced to the point where, with the imminent advent of Him Whom God will manifest, there is neither need nor place for a privileged class of clergy. Believers are encouraged to see the allegorical intent in passages of scriptures which were once viewed as references to supernatural or magical events. As God is one, so phenomenal reality is one, an organic whole animated by the Divine Will.

The contrast between this evolutionary and supremely rational conception of the nature of religious truth and that embodied by nineteenth-century Sh́'ih Islam could not have been more dramatic. Fundamental to orthodox Sh́'ism – whose full implications are today exposed in the regime of the Islamic Republic in Iran – was a literalistic understanding of the Qur'án, a preoccupation with meticulous adherence to the sharí'a, a belief that personal salvation comes through the 'imitation' (*taqlíd*) of clerical mentors, and an unbending conviction that Islam is God's final and all-sufficient revelation of truth to the world. For so static and rigid a mindset, any serious consideration of the teachings of the Báb would have unthinkable consequences.

The Báb's teachings, like the laws of the Bayán, are enunciated not in the form of an organized exposition, but lie rather embedded in the wide range of theological and mystical issues addressed in the pages of His voluminous writings. It is in the writings of Bahá'u'lláh that, as with the laws of the Bayán, these scattered truths and precepts are taken up, reshaped, and integrated into a unified, coherent system of belief. The subject lies far beyond the scope of this brief paper, but the reader will find in Bahá'u'lláh's major doctrinal work, the Kitáb-i-Íqán ('Book of Certitude'), not only echoes of the Báb's teachings, but a coherent exposition of their central concepts.

࿘

Finally, a striking feature of the Báb's writings, which has emerged as an important element of Bahá'í belief and history, is the mission envisioned for 'the peoples of the West' and admiration of the qualities that fit them for it. This, too, was in dramatic contrast to the professed contempt for *farangi* and 'infidel' thought that prevailed in the Islamic world of His time. Western scientific advancement is particularly praised, for example, as are the fairness of mind and concern for cleanliness that the Báb saw Westerners on the whole as tending to display. His appreciation is not merely generalized but touches on even such mundane matters as postal systems and printing facilities.

At the outset of the Báb's mission, the Qayyúmu'l-Asmá' called on 'the peoples of the West' to arise and leave their homes in promotion of the Day of God:

> Become as true brethren in the one and indivisible religion of God, free from distinction, for verily God desireth that your hearts should become mirrors unto your brethren in the Faith, so that ye find yourselves reflected in them, and they in you. This is the true Path of God, the Almighty. . . .*

To a British physician who treated Him for injuries inflicted during his interrogation in Tabríz, the Báb expressed His confidence that, in time, Westerners, too, would embrace the truth of His mission.

This theme is powerfully taken up in the work of Bahá'u'lláh. A series of 'tablets' called on such European rulers as Queen Victoria, Napoleon III, Kaiser Wilhelm I, and Tsar Alexander II to examine dispassionately 'the Cause of God'. The British monarch is warmly commended for the

---

* ibid. p. 56.

actions of her government in abolishing slavery throughout the empire and for the establishment of constitutional government. Perhaps the most extraordinary theme the letters contain is a summons, a virtual mandate to 'the Rulers of America and the Presidents of the Republics therein'. They are called on to 'bind . . . the broken with the hands of justice' and to 'crush the oppressor who flourisheth with the rod of the commandments of [their] Lord'.[*]

Anticipating the decisive contribution which Western lands and peoples are destined to make in founding the institutions of world order, Bahá'u'lláh wrote:

In the East the Light of His Revelation hath broken; in the West have appeared the signs of His dominion. Ponder this in your hearts, O people. . . .[†]

It was on 'Abdu'l-Bahá that responsibility devolved to lay the foundations for this distinctive feature of the missions of the Báb and Bahá'u'lláh. Visiting both Western Europe and North America in the years 1911–1913, He coupled high praise for the material accomplishments of the West with an urgent appeal that they be balanced with the essentials of 'spiritual civilization'.

During the years of World War I, after returning to the Holy Land, 'Abdu'l-Bahá drafted a series of letters addressed to the small body of Bahá'u'lláh's followers in the United States and Canada, summoning them to arise and carry the Bahá'í message to the remotest corners of the globe. As soon as international conditions permitted, these Bahá'ís began to respond. Their example has since been followed by

---

* Bahá'u'lláh, *The Kitáb-i-Aqdas*, para. 88.
† Bahá'u'lláh, *Tablets of Bahá'u'lláh revealed after the Kitáb-i-Aqdas* (Wilmette, IL: Bahá'í Publishing Trust, 1988), p. 13.

members of the many other Bahá'í communities around the world which have proliferated during subsequent decades.

To the North American believers, too, 'Abdu'l-Bahá confided the task of laying the foundations of the democratically elected institutions conceived by Bahá'u'lláh for the administration of the affairs of the Bahá'í community. The entire decision-making structure of the present-day administrative system of the Faith at local, national, and international levels, had its origins in these simple consultative assemblies formed by the American and Canadian believers.

Bahá'ís see a parallel pattern of response to the Divine mandate, however unrecognized, in the growing leadership Western nations have assumed throughout the present century in the efforts to bring about global peace. This is particularly true of the endeavor to inaugurate a system of international order. For his own vision in this respect, as well as for the lonely courage that the effort to realize it required, 'the immortal Woodrow Wilson' won an enduring place of honor in the writings of the Guardian of the Bahá'í Faith.

Bahá'ís are likewise aware that it has been such governments as those of Europe, the United States, Canada, and Australia which have taken the lead in the field of human rights. The Bahá'í community has experienced at first hand the benefits of this concern in the successful interventions undertaken on behalf of its members in Iran during the recurrent persecutions under the regimes of the Pahlavi shahs and the Islamic Republic.

Nothing of what has been said should suggest an uncritical admiration of European or North American cultures on the part of either the Báb or Bahá'u'lláh nor an endorsement of the ideological foundations on which they rest. Far otherwise. Bahá'u'lláh warns in ominous tones of the suffering and ruin that will be visited upon the entire human race if Western civilization continues on its course of excess. During His visits to Europe and America, 'Abdu'l-Bahá called on His hearers in poignant language to free themselves, while time still remained, from racial and national prejudices, as well as materialistic preoccupations, whose unappreciated dangers, He said, threatened the future of their nations and of all humankind.

ço

Today, a century and a half after the Báb's mission was inaugurated, the influence of His life and words has found expression in a global community drawn from every background on earth. The first act of most Bahá'í pilgrims on their arrival at the World Centre of their Faith is to walk up the flower-bordered avenue leading to the exquisite Shrine housing the Báb's mortal remains, and to lay their foreheads on the threshold of His resting place. They confidently believe that, in future years, 'pilgrim kings' will reverently ascend the magnificent terraced staircase rising from the foot of the 'Mountain of God' to the Shrine's entrance, and place the emblems of their authority at this same threshold. In the countries from which the pilgrims come, countless children from every background and every language today bear the names of the Báb's martyred companions – Ṭáhirih, Quddús, Ḥusayn, Zaynab, Vaḥíd, Anís – much as children throughout the lands of the Roman empire began 2,000 years ago to carry the unfamiliar Hebrew names of the disciples of Jesus Christ.

Bahá'u'lláh's choice of a resting place for the body of His Forerunner – brought with infinite difficulty from Persia – itself holds great significance for the Bahá'í world. Throughout history the blood of martyrs has been 'the seed of faith'. In the age that is witnessing the gradual unification of humankind, the blood of the Bábí martyrs has become the seed not merely of personal faith, but of the administrative institutions which are, in the words of Shoghi Effendi, 'the nucleus [and] the very pattern' of the World Order conceived by Bahá'u'lláh.[*] The relationship is symbolized by the supreme position that the Shrine of the Báb occupies in the progressive development of the administrative center of the Bahá'í Faith on Mount Carmel.

Few there must be among the stream of Bahá'í pilgrims entering these majestic surroundings today whose minds do not turn to the familiar words in which the Báb said farewell 150 years ago to the handful of His first followers, all of them bereft of influence or wealth and most of them destined, as He was, soon to lose their lives:

> The secret of the Day that is to come is now concealed. It can neither be divulged nor estimated. The newly born babe of that Day excels the wisest and most venerable men of this time, and the lowliest and most unlearned of that period shall surpass in understanding the most erudite and accomplished divines of this age. Scatter throughout the length and breadth of this land, and, with steadfast feet and sanctified hearts, prepare the way for His coming. Heed not your weaknesses and frailty; fix your gaze upon the invincible power of the Lord, your God, the Almighty. . . . Arise in His name, put your trust wholly in Him, and be assured of ultimate victory.[†]

---

[*] *The World Order of Bahá'u'lláh*, p. 144.
[†] *The Dawn-Breakers*, p. 94.

First published in the 1932–34 edition of The Bahá'í World
*(Vol. V), this essay by Mary Maxwell – later known as 'Amatu'l-
Bahá Rúḥíyyih Khánum – reflected on the dominant themes
of* The Dawn-Breakers, *the early narrative of Bábí history
authored by Nabíl-i-Zarandí.*

The Re-florescence of Historical Romance in Nabíl

One of the most inspiring things about Nabíl's Narrative,
The Dawn-Breakers, is that it creates, not alone a background of knowledge and authenticity in which to set the
Bahá'í Cause in its present world-wide expression, nor just
a key to a 'way' of living and being that we in the West had
almost forgotten was possible to the human race, (latent
indeed within their seed of humanness), but opens before
us a stage which was a nation and an epoch in history, on
which a pageant of romance, of adventure and heroism
unequaled by any crusade plays itself before us. And slowly
as we become more *en rapport* with the thought and mode
of expression of Nabíl, that pageant and its figures begin
to take hold on us, to live for us as realisms; or perhaps
something deeper still, we take hold of them and, inspired
by their deeds and the lofty atmosphere of their lives, try to
carry out into our own far Western World that same banner
of shining belief and inner conviction that they raised aloft
in Persia not eighty years ago.

The mere sound of their names is music to us; their faces,
in which the light of their actions shone so brightly, become
stars in the new world dawn, casting forever their radiance
upon the path of men. The dusty roads of Persia, winding
amidst its rocky hills and wind and heat-swept plains,
become familiar highways in our minds down which we
follow, with love and tender adoration, the green-turbaned,

slight figure of the Báb led by his cavalcade of guards who loved Him so devotedly they begged Him to escape from their custody. Or we accompany Qurratu'l-'Ayn in her howdah, travelling from city to city and raising a call no woman had ever dared to proclaim before in the lands of her bondage. Or it is after the hoofs of Mullá Ḥusayn's horse that we speed, hearing him cry, 'Yá Ṣáhibu'z-Zamán!' shaking the very walls of our hearts.

In Nabíl we partake of the food of beauty, a rare thing in a world grown clouded with strife, terror and sadness. We see the days rise under the light of a heavy golden sun, in a land where the weight of its heat falls on the world like a tangible cloak; we await the nights under an Eastern sky where when the moon is absent a million stars hang low to light your way, and when the moon is present she eclipses in white light all but her own deep and mysterious shadows. Against these settings rise the nineteen Letters of the Living.

The first, the Báb. No one person could attempt an adequate description of that blessed Youth, but through the book run testimonies of Him, as though He were a wind in the tree of humanity and the voices of the leaves each gave their separate praise to Him. '. . . His countenance revealed an expression of humility and kindliness which I can never describe.' 'Every time I met Him, I found Him in such a state of humility and lowliness as words fail me to describe; His downcast eyes, His extreme courtesy, and the serene expression of His face made an indelible impression upon my soul.' 'The sweetness of His utterance still lingers in my memory.' 'The melody of His chanting, the rhythmic flow of the verses which streamed from His lips caught our ears and penetrated into our very souls . . . Our hearts vibrated in their depths to the appeal of His utterance.' Not alone did every bearing of that One give forth testimony of His station, but His walk was sufficient for Quddús to distinguish Him. 'Why seek you to hide Him from me?' he exclaimed. 'I can recognize Him by His gait. I confidently testify that none besides Him, whether in the East or in the West, can claim to be the Truth. None other can manifest the power and majesty that radiate from His holy person.'

After passing from one persecution to another, and prison to prison, always with that surpassing meekness of mien, the glory of the light within Him was turned like a beacon upon the world when He declared His station to the 'ulamás of Tabríz at His trial. He entered that room where all were arrayed against Him, and they were but the symbols of the nation which would at length kill Him and seek to hound from the earth His teachings and His followers, and that nation in turn was only the voice of a darkened world which perished from His light. And yet, 'the majesty of His gait, the expression of overpowering coherence which sat upon His brow – above all, the spirit of power which shone from His whole being, appeared to have for a moment crushed the soul out of the body of those whom He had greeted. A deep, a mysterious silence, suddenly fell upon them. Not one soul in that distinguished assembly dared breathe a single word. At last the stillness which brooded over them was broken by the Niẓámu'l-'Ulamá'. "Who do you claim to be," he asked the Báb, "and what is the message which you have brought?" "I am," thrice exclaimed the Báb, "I am, I am, the promised One! I am the One whose name you have for a thousand years invoked, at whose mention you have risen, whose advent you have longed to witness, and the hour of whose Revelation you have prayed God to hasten. Verily I say, it is incumbent upon the peoples of both the East and the West to obey My word and to pledge allegiance to My person."'

Thus did God's paean rise in this greatest dawn of history, summoning a world to the shores of His Communion. In Bahá'u'lláh's own Words: 'Nigh unto the celestial paradise a new garden hath been made manifest, round which circle the denizens of the realm on high and the immortal dwellers of the exalted paradise. Strive then that ye may attain that station, that ye may unravel from its wind-flowers the mysteries of love and know from its eternal fruit the secret of divine and consummate wisdom.'

What was the fragrance of those 'windflowers'? No faint perfume of abstinence, no celibate fragrance that retired from the world, but a deep and abiding passion of being. A love that burned like a fire in the hearts of the souls and they became as stubble in its flame. Their lives *were* romance, sacrifice, love, and a deep and mysterious joy. Were they not – those who bared their breasts to the seen and unseen shafts of the enemy – like that whale of love that swallows up the seven seas and says, 'Is there yet any more?' and like that lover – 'thou wilt see him cool in fire and find him dry even in the sea.' When the heroes of Shaykh Ṭabarsí had been reduced to starving to death on the bone dust of their horses, grass, and their saddle and shoe leather, did not Quddús say, while rolling a cannon-ball scornfully with his foot: 'How utterly unaware are these boastful aggressors of the power of God's avenging wrath! . . . Fear not the threats of the wicked, neither be dismayed by the clamour of the ungodly.' Then he continued, saying that no power on earth could hasten or postpone the hour of their death, but should they allow themselves for one moment to become afraid they would have cast themselves out of the stronghold of Divine protection. Bahá'u'lláh said: 'My love is My stronghold; he that entereth therein is safe and secure, and he that turneth away shall surely stray and perish.' When we have followed Nabíl's Narrative to the last of its multiple truths, histories and wisdoms, we find that the key to it, to the lives of those early Bábí martyrs, nay to the Cause of the Báb and Bahá'u'lláh, is summed up in the mystery of love. Their love was their indomitable and miraculous strength, their shining armour of protection, the diadem of their faith, the blood in which they pledged their eternal Beloved – that One for whom the heart of the world has ever languished and sought.

Nabíl becomes a lyric poet in those lines in which he describes the love of Bahá'u'lláh and the Báb. 'The Báb, whose trials and sufferings had preceded, in almost every case, those of Bahá'u'lláh, had offered Himself to ransom His Beloved from the perils that beset that precious Life; whilst Bahá'u'lláh, on His part, unwilling that He who so greatly loved Him should be the sole Sufferer, shared at every turn the cup that had touched His lips. Such love no eye has ever beheld, nor has mortal heart conceived such mutual devotion. If the branches of every tree were turned into pens, and all the seas into ink, and earth and heaven rolled into one parchment, the immensity of that love would still remain unexplored, and the depths of that devotion unfathomed.'

Our minds turn to Mullá Ḥusayn, who, mounted at the head of two hundred companions, bearing the prophesied Black Standard of Muḥammad, and wearing the Báb's green turban, held at bay the combined armies of the Sháh for eleven months. Riding out in the teeth of twelve thousand men and crying, 'O Lord of the Age,' he and the invincible host of God's followers dispersed the terrified enemy. At length he shed his blood at Quddús' feet whilst speaking of the depths of the Sea of Revelation and their beloved Báb, ere his life ebbed away.

Or we remember Qurratu'l-'Ayn, beautiful and famous, who escaped clandestinely from her own home in which her husband had imprisoned her in his opposition to her Bábí Faith, leaving her children motherless and making their father her bitterest enemy, to arise and proclaim throughout Persia and 'Iráq the glory of the New Day. She created such a furor throughout the East that E. G. Browne was compelled to pay her one of the most glowing tributes woman has ever received. 'The appearance of such a woman as Qurratu'l-'Ayn is in any country and any age a rare phenomenon, but in such a country as Persia it is a prodigy – nay, almost a miracle. Alike in virtue of her marvellous beauty, her rare intellectual gifts, her fervid eloquence, her fearless devotion, and her glorious martyrdom, she stands forth incomparable and immortal, amongst her countrywomen. Had the Bábí Religion no other claim to greatness this were sufficient – that it produced a heroine like Qurratu'l-'Ayn.' The queenly names of history fade before the unveiled beauty of 'her whom the tongue of power hath named Tahirih – the pure one.' That moment, when, with one gesture of freeing herself and all women from the veils of weakness, inferiority, and submission, Qurratu'l-'Ayn and the Bábí men unveiled, is unrivaled and has no precedent. Some turned from her bared face and doubted the Messenger of God because of tradition; one old man, unable to bear the age in which he found himself, attempted suicide; Quddús was spellbound with indignation; but Qurratu'l-'Ayn cast her glance towards Bahá'u'lláh, who had named her 'Ṭahirih,' and said: '"Verily, amid gardens and rivers shall the pious dwell in the seat of truth, in the presence of the potent King." . . . This day is the day of festivity and universal rejoicing, the day on which the fetters of the past are burst asunder. Let those who have shared in this great achievement arise and embrace each other.' And they feasted together in the tent of Bahá'u'lláh, surrounded by the beautiful gardens of Bada<u>sh</u>t.

The same quality of beauty and majesty pervades all the events chronicled by Nabíl; sincerity is all that is required to become deeply and permanently inspired by the record contained in *The Dawn-Breakers*, for no heart who loved truth could read its history unmoved and remain unchanged. Here one tastes again those 'living waters' that alone can revivify mankind and nurture in him the seed of immortality.

Even the humblest of souls won undying glory, like that man who, seated in the bazaars of Iṣfáhán, heard the proclamation of the Báb's message while sifting his wheat, and instantly and unhesitatingly accepted it. Later he hastened, sieve in hand, to join the heroes of Ṭabarsí, saying, 'With this sieve which I carry with me I intend to sift the people in every city through which I pass. Whomsoever I find ready to espouse the Cause I have embraced, I will ask to join me and hasten forthwith to the field of martyrdom.' Of all the wise and devout of that city he alone received the crown of a martyr's fame.

And there was that heart-shattered boy who, when in Tabríz, heard of the Blessed Báb, longed to speed to Him and offer his life in the lists of His followers, and was imprisoned by his family who thought that if not already bewitched, one glimpse of the Báb would enchant him permanently as it did thousands. Inconsolable, he languished and pined for the only expression that could ever satisfy his pure young soul. The agony of his longing was rewarded when in a vision he saw the Báb, who addressed to him these words: 'Rejoice, the hour is approaching when, in this very city, I shall be suspended before the eyes of the multitude and shall fall a victim to the fire of the enemy, I shall choose no one but you to share with me the cup of martyrdom. Rest assured that this promise I give you shall be fulfilled.' A few years later it was this youth's head that rested on the heart of the Báb as they hung bound from the walls of the barrack square of Tabríz, and it was his flesh that was inextricably interwoven with the Báb's remains after their joint execution.

To some Nabíl will be a fascinating historical document. To others, great literature. Some will feel crushed by the tragedy of the brutally sacrificed lives of thousands. Others will be exalted by the knowledge that again the human soul has risen to its greatest heights and men have died immortal deaths. But to all of these its more subtile fragrance will be lost. Only those who have through some experience in life touched to their lips the cup of divine love, will fully grasp the purport of this mighty pageant. They will know why the martyrs sometimes sang when being led to execution: 'Happy he whom love's intoxication So hath overcome that scarce he knows Whether at the feet of the Beloved It be head or turban which he throws!'

And they, becoming fired with that same zeal that pervaded those Dawn-Breakers, will carry on and establish that vision of hope for the world, for which they died.

6

OTHER VOICES

Other Voices

You ask me for some particulars of my interview with the founder of the sect known as Bábís. Nothing of any importance transpired in this interview, as the Báb was aware of my having been sent with two other Persian doctors to see whether he was of sane mind or merely a madman, to decide the question whether to put him to death or not. With this knowledge he was loth to answer any questions put to him. To all enquiries he merely regarded us with a mild look, chanting in a low melodious voice some hymns, I suppose . . . He only once deigned to answer me, on my saying that I was not a Musulmán and was willing to know something about his religion, as I might perhaps be inclined to adopt it. He regarded me very intently on my saying this, and replied that he had no doubt of all Europeans coming over to his religion. Our report to the Sháh at that time was of a nature to spare his life. He was put to death some time after by the order of the Amír-i-Nizám Mírzá Taqí Khán.

On our report he merely got the bastinado, in which operation a farrásh, whether intentionally or not, struck him across the face with the stick destined for his feet, which produced a great wound and swelling of the face. On being asked whether a Persian surgeon should be brought to treat him, he expressed a desire that I should be sent for, and I accordingly treated him for a few days, but in the interviews consequent on this I could never get him to have a confidential chat with me, as some Government people were always present, he being a prisoner.

He was very thankful for my attentions to him. He was a very mild and delicate-looking man, rather small in stature and very fair for a Persian, with a melodious soft voice, which struck me much. Being a Sayyid, he was dressed in the habits of that sect, as were also his two companions. In fact his whole look and deportment went far to dispose one in his favour. Of his doctrine I heard nothing from his own lips, although the idea was that there existed in his religion a certain approach to Christianity. He was seen by some Armenian carpenters, who were sent to make some repairs in his prison, reading the Bible, and he took no pains to conceal it, but on the contrary told them of it. Most assuredly the Musulmán fanaticism does not exist in his religion, as applied to Christians, nor is there that restraint of females that now exists.[46]

Dr William Cormick

❧

. . . who can fail to be attracted by the gentle spirit of Mírzá 'Alí Muhammad? His sorrowful and persecuted life; his purity of conduct, and youth; his courage and uncomplaining patience under misfortune; his complete self-negation; the dim ideal of a better state of things which can be discerned through the obscure and mystic utterances of the Beyán; but most of all his tragic death, all serve to enlist our sympathies on behalf of the young prophet of Shíráz. The irresistible charm which won him such devotion during his life still lives on, and still continues to influence the minds of the Persian people.[47]

Edward G. Browne

❧

To the Western observer . . . it is the complete sincerity of the Bábís, their fearless disregard of death and torture undergone for the sake of their religion, their certain conviction as to the truth of their faith, their generally admirable conduct towards mankind, and especially towards their fellow believers, which constitute their strongest claim on his attention.[48]

Edward G. Browne

✴

I trust that I have told you enough to make it clear that the objects at which this religion aims are neither trivial nor unworthy of the noble self-devotion and heroism of the Founder and his followers. It is the lives and deaths of these, their hope which knows no despair, their love which knows no cooling, their steadfastness which knows no wavering, which stamp this wonderful movement with a character entirely its own. For whatever may be the merits or demerits of the doctrines for which these scores and hundreds of our fellow-men died, they have at least found something which made them ready to

> leave all things under the sky,
> And go forth naked under sun and rain,
> And work and wait and watch out all their years.

It is not a small or easy thing to endure what these have endured, and surely what they deemed worth life itself is worth trying to understand. I say nothing of the mighty influence which, as I believe, the Bábí faith will exert in the future, nor of the new life it may perchance breathe into a dead people; for, whether it succeed or fail, the splendid heroism of the Bábí martyrs is a thing eternal and indestructible.

He whose soul by love is quickened never can to death
  be hurled;
Written is their life immortal in the records of the world.

But what I cannot hope to have conveyed to you is the
terrible earnestness of these men, and the indescribable
influence which this earnestness, combined with other
qualities, exerts on any one who has actually been brought
in contact with them. That you must take my word for, or
else –

Chú dar rah bi-bíní burídé sarí,
Ki ghaltán shavad sú-ye-meydán-i-má,
Asú purs, asú purs asrár-i-má,
Kasú bishnaví sirr-i-panhán-i-má.

When thou seest in the path a severed head
Which is rolling towards our field,
Ask of it, ask of it our secrets,
For from it thou may'st hear our hidden mystery.
    (From the *Díván* of Shams-i-Tabríz)[49]

Edward G. Browne

☙

Such a prophet was the Báb; we call him 'prophet' for want
of a better name; 'yea, I say unto you, a prophet and more
than a prophet.' His combination of mildness and power
is so rare that we have to place him in a line with super-
normal men . . . We learn that, at great points in his career,
after he had been in an ecstasy, such radiance of might and
majesty, streamed from his countenance that none could
bear to look upon the effulgence of his glory and beauty.

Nor was it an uncommon occurrence for unbelievers invol-
untarily to bow down in lowly obeisance on beholding His
Holiness . . .

The gentle spirit of the Báb is surely high up in the cycles
of eternity. Who can fail, as Professor Browne says, to be
attracted by him?[50]

Thomas K. Cheyne

ↄ

This movement had been started by Mírzá 'Alí Muḥammad,
a young merchant of Shiráz who in the forties of the last
century appeared as the Prophet of a religion reform-
ing Islám and very soon found numerous followers. He
proclaimed that the Almighty is the Knowledge and he
is the Gate (Báb) through which truth and faith can be
approached. The tyrannical government of Persia did not
permit any trifling with the question of reformation. They
not only executed with exceptional cruelty the 'Gate of
God,' but sent more than twenty thousand men, women
and children to martyrdom. It is, however, an eternal experience that the earth does not drink the blood of martyrs
without leaving great traces.[51]

Rusztem Vámbéry

ↄ

There exists the Bábí sect whose religious teachings are of
a very high order . . . The members of this sect recognize
no external form of religion, and the basis of religion is,
according to them, the goodness of life, that is to say, love
for one's neighbour, and non-participation in the evil pro-
jects carried out by governments . . .

Bábísm . . . is one of the highest forms and purest of religious teachings.

I have known about the Bábís for a long time, and am much interested in their teachings. It seems to me that these teachings, like all rationalist, social and religious teachings . . . have a great future, above all because they have rejected all these monstrous hierarchies which divide the old religions, and they aspire to come together into one single religion common to the whole of mankind. That is why the Bábí teachings, insofar as they reject the old Muslim superstitions and do not establish any new ones . . . and insofar as they hold fast to their main and fundamental ideas of brother-hood, equality and love, are assured a great future . . .

. . . I sympathize will all my heart with Bábísm, insofar as it preaches brotherhood and equality between all men, and the sacrifice of material life in the service of God.[52]

Count Leo Tolstoy

છ

Tales of magnificent heroism illumine the bloodstained pages of Babi history. Ignorant and unlettered as many of its votaries are, and have been, they are yet prepared to die for their religion, and fires of Smithfield did not kindle a nobler courage than has met and defied the more refined torture-mongers of Tihran. Of no small account, then, must be the tenets of a creed that can awaken in its followers so rare and beautiful a spirit of self-sacrifice . . .

From the facts that Babism in its earliest years found itself in conflict with the civil powers and that an attempt was made by Babis upon the life of the Shah, it has been wrongly inferred that the movement was political in origin and Nihilist in character. It does not appear from a study of the writings either of the Bab or his successors, that there is any foundation for such a suspicion. The persecution of the government very early drove the adherents of the new creed into an attitude of rebellion; and in the exasperation produced by the struggle and by the ferocious brutality with which the rights of conquest were exercised by the victors, it was not surprising if fanatical hands were found ready to strike the sovereign down. At the present time the Babis are equally loyal with any other subjects of the Crown. Nor does there appear any greater justice in the charges of socialism, communism, and immorality, that have so freely been levelled at the youthful persuasion. . . The charge of immorality seems to have arisen partly from the malignant inventions of opponents, partly from the much greater freedom claimed for women by the Bab, which in the oriental mind is scarcely dissociable from profligacy of conduct . . .

Broadly regarded, Babism may be defined as a creed of charity, and almost of common humanity. Brotherly love, kindness to children, courtesy combined with dignity, sociability, hospitality, freedom from bigotry, friendliness even to Christians, are included in its tenets . . .[53]

George Nathaniel Curzon

ఌ

The story of the Bab . . . was the story of spiritual heroism unsurpassed . . . That a youth of no social influence and no education should, by the simple power of insight, be able to pierce into the heart of things and see the real truth, and then hold on to it with such firmness of conviction and present it with such suasion that he was able to convince men that he was the Messiah and get them to follow him to

death itself, was one of those splendid facts in human history
. . . The Bab's passionate sincerity could not be doubted, for
he had given his life for his faith. And that there must be
something in his message that appealed to men and satisfied
their souls was witnessed to by the fact that thousands gave
their lives in his cause and millions now follow him.

If a young man could, in only six years of ministry, by the
sincerity of his purpose and the attraction of his personality,
so inspire rich and poor, cultured and illiterate, alike with
belief in himself and his doctrines that they would remain
staunch though hunted down and without trial sentenced
to death, sawn asunder, strangled, shot, blown from guns;
and if men of high position and culture in Persia, Turkey
and Egypt in numbers to this day adhere to his doctrines;
his life must be one of those events in the last hundred years
which is really worthy of study . . .

And the ideal community which the Bab had in mind
was one which would be characterised by brotherly love; by
dignity combined with courtesy in all dealings and transac-
tions between its members; by the cultivation of all useful
arts and improvements; . . . by the amelioration of the
condition of women, who were to be allowed to appear in
society; by general elementary education; by provision for
the poor out of the common treasury; by the treatment of
children with kindness and affection and allowing them to
play and enjoy themselves.

. . . He had before him the task – the same as all religious
reformers have and always will have – of getting men who
are *set* and settled in long established ways of life to change
those ways. He had to get them radically to change their
whole attitude to life. They and their fathers before them for
generations back had pinned their faith on certain formulas.
He wanted them to change those formulas for others. And

for such a task not only the most patient loving-kindness was required, but the most perfect grace. He must not only be a lover of his kind, he must be an artist with infinite delicacy of touch in the representation of his views.

Outwardly, men in every country and in every age have been indifferent to religion. But though outwardly indifferent they are in truth highly sensitive to any disturbance of their religious beliefs, and they spring into action directly they are threatened. This religious reformers have to expect and prepare for. Opposition should be to them a sign that religion is alive and not dead. They have to abate not a tittle of their zeal. But they have to exercise patience, forbearance and sympathy – enter into the feelings of their opponents and present their message with such winning grace that the opponents are able to see that it means nothing injurious to the good that is in them, but may be a means of making the good better.

The Bab, in the conditions in which he had to work, might still have lost his life in the process. But of his life he thought nothing. His life was only a small part of himself. His self was his message. His message it was that he wanted to be effective long after his death . . .[54]

Sir Francis Younghusband

ᴄᴏ

Thousands of martyrs rushed to death for him with joyful alacrity. The great butchery of his followers at Teheran was a scene perhaps unparalleled in history. 'That day in the streets and bazaars of Teheran,' says an eye-witness, 'the residents will never forget. To this moment when it is talked of, the mingled wonder and horror which the citizens then experienced appears unabated by the lapse of years. They saw women and children walking forward between their executioners, with great gashes all over their bodies and burning matches thrust into the wounds. The victims were dragged along by ropes, and hurried on by strokes of the whip. Children and women went singing a verse to this effect, "Verily we came from God, and to him shall we return!" Their shrill voices rose loud and clear in the profound silence of the multitude. If one of these poor wretches fell down, and the guards forced him up again with blows or bayonet-thrusts, as he staggered on with the blood trickling down every limb, he would spend his remaining energy in dancing and crying in an access of zeal, "Verily we are God's, and to him we return!" Some of the children expired on the way. The executioners threw their corpses in front of their fathers and their sisters, who yet marched proudly on, giving hardly a second glance. At the place of execution life was offered them if they would abjure, but to no purpose. One of the condemned was informed that unless he recanted, the throats of his two sons should be cut upon his own bosom. The eldest of these little boys was fourteen years old, and they stood red with their own blood and with their flesh burned and blistered, calmly listening to the dialogue. The father, stretching himself upon the earth, answered that he was ready; and the oldest boy, eagerly claiming his birthright, asked to be murdered first. At length all was over; night closed in upon heaps of mangled carcasses; the heads were suspended in bunches on the scaffold, and the dogs . . . gathered in troops from every side as darkness veiled the awful scene.'

This happened in 1852. In the reign of Khosrow I, the sect of Mazdak was smothered in blood in the same way. Absolute devotion is to simple natures the most exquisite of enjoyments, and, in fact, a necessity. In the Bábí persecution,

people who had hardly joined the sect came and denounced
themselves, that they might suffer with the rest. It is so sweet
to mankind to suffer for something, that the allurement of
martyrdom is itself often enough to inspire faith. A disciple
who shared the tortures of Báb, hanging by his side on the
ramparts of Tabríz and awaiting a lingering death, had only
one word to say – 'Are you pleased with me, Master?'[55]

Ernest Renan

❧

From that subtle race issues the most remarkable movement which modern Muḥammadanism has produced. . . .
Disciples gathered round him, and the movement was not
checked by his arrest, his imprisonment for nearly six years
and his final execution in 1850. . . . It, too, claims to be a
universal teaching; it has already its noble army of martyrs
and its holy books; has Persia, in the midst of her miseries,
given birth to a religion which will go round the world?[56]

Joseph Estlin Carpenter

BIOGRAPHICAL NOTES

Bahá'u'lláh (1817–1892)

Born Mírzá Ḥusayn-'Alí Núrí in Tehran, Iran, Bahá'u'lláh ('The Glory of God') was a Manifestation of God and the Founder of the Bahá'í Faith. Bahá'u'lláh became a follower of the Báb in 1845. In 1853, Bahá'u'lláh was exiled to Baghdad for his allegiance to the Báb. Ten years later, He publicly declared Himself to be 'He whom God shall make manifest', the Messianic figure heralded by the Báb. Further exiles within the Ottoman empire followed – to Constantinople, Adrianople and finally to the prison city of Akka. Bahá'u'lláh penned more than 100 volumes of Writings elucidating His Teachings on the unity of God, religion and humanity, and detailing the institutions and measures required to establish a global civilization.

'Abdu'l-Bahá (1844–1921)

The eldest son of Bahá'u'lláh, 'Abdu'l-Bahá was His Father's appointed successor as Head of the Bahá'í Faith from 1892 until 1921. Sharing in Bahá'u'lláh's banishments and exiles from 1853 onwards, 'Abdu'l-Bahá remained a prisoner in Akka until he was released following the Young Turks Revolution in 1908. He then made a number of extended journeys to Egypt and the West to promote the Bahá'í message and international peace. During His lifetime,

'Abdu'l-Bahá was renowned as an exemplary human being, and the leading exponent of a new Faith.

Shoghi Effendi (1897–1957)

Shoghi Effendi Rabbání was the Guardian of the Bahá'í Faith following the passing of his Grandfather, 'Abdu'l-Bahá, in 1921. He was educated at Balliol College, Oxford, where he mastered the English language in order to be able to serve as 'Abdu'l-Bahá's secretary, and translate the Bahá'í Writings. As the Guardian, appointed by 'Abdu'l-Bahá in His Will and Testament, Shoghi Effendi was given the authority to interpret the writings of the Báb, Bahá'u'lláh and 'Abdu'l-Bahá. He spent 36 years systematically nurturing the development, deepening the understanding, and strengthening the unity of the Bahá'í community, as it increasingly grew to reflect the diversity of the entire human race.

Bábí and Bahá'í authors

Hasan Balyuzi (1908–1980) was an Afnán, a descendent of the Báb's family. Balyúzi was born in Shiraz, Iran and moved to Britain in 1932. He served on the National Spiritual Assembly of the Bahá'ís of the British Isles from 1933 to 1958, worked in the Persian section of the British Broadcasting Corporation, wrote numerous scholarly articles and books, and was appointed a Hand of the Cause of God by Shoghi Effendi in 1957.

Sara Louisa, Lady Blomfield (1859–1939) was born Sara Louisa Ryan in Co. Tipperary, Ireland. She was a distinguished early member of the Bahá'í Faith in London, and a vigorous supporter of the rights of children and women.

After encountering the Bahá'í teachings in 1907, Blomfield became one of its most outstanding proponents. She was 'Abdu'l-Bahá's host during his visits to London and a founding supporter of the Save the Children Fund after World War I. Her book *The Chosen Highway* is a much-loved chronicle of the history of the Bahá'í Faith.

Hushmand Fathe'azam (1924–2013) was born into a Bahá'í family in Tehran, Iran. After serving as secretary to the National Spiritual Assembly of the Bahá'ís of India and director of the Bahá'í Publishing Trust in New Delhi, he was elected to the Universal House of Justice in 1963 and served until 2003. His introduction to the Baha'i Faith, *The New Garden*, has been translated into more than 100 languages.

John Ferraby (1914–1973) was born in Southsea, England. He encountered the Bahá'í Faith in 1941. Within a year, he was serving on the Local Spiritual Assembly of the Bahá'ís of London and the National Spiritual Assembly of the Bahá'ís of the British Isles, becoming its secretary in 1946. From 1951 to 1956 he supported the work of opening of various territories in Africa to the Bahá'í Faith. Meeting Shoghi Effendi in 1955, Ferraby was inspired and encouraged to write his book *All Things Made New*. He was appointed a Hand of the Cause of God in 1957.

Mary Hanford Ford (1856–1937) was a writer, lecturer, and outspoken advocate of women's suffrage. She discovered the Bahá'í Faith in the early years of the twentieth century and helped form the first community of Bahá'ís in Boston. In 1910 she started writing Bahá'í books such as *The Oriental Rose*. She travelled with 'Abdu'l-Bahá during parts of his journeys in Europe and North America.

Robert Hayden (1913–1980) was a poet, essayist, and educator. He served as Consultant in Poetry to the Library of Congress from 1976 to 1978, a role today known as US Poet Laureate. He was the first African-American writer to hold the office. He embraced the Baháʼí Faith in 1943.

Horace Holley (1887–1960) was born in Torrington, Connecticut. He was introduced to the Baháʼí Faith in 1909, and later served as a member and secretary of the National Spiritual Assembly of the Baháʼís of the United States and Canada. A gifted poet and prolific essayist, he was appointed by Shoghi Effendi as a Hand of the Cause of God in 1951 and later elected as one of the nine Custodians who acted as the Chief Stewards of the Faith from 1957 to 1963, following the passing of Shoghi Effendi and prior to the first election of the Universal House of Justice.

Douglas Martin (1929–) is a Canadian historian and writer. He served as a member of the Universal House of Justice from 1993–2003.

Mary Maxwell (1910–2000) best known by the title Amatuʼl-Bahá Rúḥíyyih Khánum, was the wife of Shoghi Effendi. She was appointed by him as a Hand of the Cause of God. A prolific writer, she was the author of several published books, such as *Prescription for Living* and *The Priceless Pearl*. After Shoghi Effendi's passing in 1957, she travelled extensively, promoting the Baháʼí teachings around the world and encouraging nascent Baháʼí communities.

Nabíl-i-Aʻẓam (Muhammad-i-Zarandí) (d. 1892) was a poet and historian. Shoghi Effendi translated into English 'Nabíl's Narrative of the Early Days of the Baháʼí Revelation', and published it as *The Dawn-Breakers*. Nabíl was named by the Guardian as an 'Apostle of Bahá'u'lláh'.

A. L. M. Nicolas (1864–1939) was a French orientalist and consular official whose study of the life of the Báb and translations of important Bábí texts are of singular importance. He contributed regularly to journals, especially the *Revue du Monde Musulman*.

George Townshend (1876–1957) was born in Dublin, Ireland, and was a well-known writer and clergyman. He spent many years near Ballinasloe, County Galway, where he was incumbent of Ahascragh and Archdeacon of Clonfert. He later became the Canon of St. Patrick's Cathedral in Dublin. He recognized the Bahá'í Faith in 1921. However, it was not until reaching the age of 70 that Townshend renounced his orders to the Anglican Church and wrote a pamphlet to all Christians, *The Old Churches and the New World Faith*, proclaiming his allegiance to the Bahá'í religion. In 1951, he was named a Hand of the Cause of God by Shoghi Effendi, who greatly admired Townshend's literary capabilities.

Other voices

Edward Granville Browne (1862–1926) was born in Gloucestershire, England. Browne made an extended visit to Iran after being made a Fellow of Pembroke College, Cambridge. He researched subjects which few other Western scholars had explored, many of them related to Persian history and literature. He published two translations of Bábí histories, including *A Traveller's Narrative* by 'Abdu'l-Bahá, and wrote several of the few Western accounts of early Bábí and Bahá'í history. He left a vivid pen-portrait of his meetings with Bahá'u'lláh in 1890.

Joseph Estlin Carpenter (1844–1927) was a Unitarian minister, the principal of Manchester College, Oxford, and a pioneer in the study of comparative religion.

Thomas Kelly Cheyne (1841–1915) was an English divine and Biblical critic. He consistently urged in his writings the necessity of a broad and comprehensive study of the scriptures in the light of literary, historical and scientific considerations. He was visited by 'Abdu'l-Bahá in Oxford in December 1912. Cheyne's book on the Bahá'í Faith, *The Reconciliation of Races and Religions*, was published in 1914.

Dr William Cormick (1822–1877), the Iranian-born son of an Irish physician and his Armenian wife, was a medical doctor to the British mission in Tabríz. In 1848, when the Báb was tried before a tribunal of religious and civil authorities, Cormick was assigned to determine His sanity. After the Báb was subjected to the bastinado – a severe beating of the soles of the feet – He asked to be treated by Cormick, the only Westerner known to have met the Báb. His description of their encounter was sent in a letter to an American missionary friend.

George Nathaniel Curzon (1859–1925) was a British Conservative statesman, who served as Viceroy of India from 1899 to 1905, and as Secretary of State for Foreign Affairs from 1919 to 1924. He spent several months in Persia during 1889/1890, writing *Persia and the Persian Question* in 1892, and several articles on the country and its political environment for *The Times* newspaper.

Ernest Renan (1823–1892) was a French philosopher, expert of Semitic languages and civilizations, historian and writer. He is best known for his influential historical works on early Christianity, and his political theories, especially concerning nationalism and national identity.

Count Leo Tolstoy (1828–1910) was one of the greatest novelists of all time, best known for *War and Peace* and *Anna Karenina*. In the 1870s, Tolstoy experienced a profound moral crisis, followed by what he regarded as an equally profound spiritual awakening, as outlined in his non-fiction work *A Confession*. Tolstoy's essays on religion and educational reform made him an influential and controversial figure in Russian history.

Rusztem Vámbéry (1872–1942), a judge, politician, and criminologist, was the son of the distinguished Jewish-Hungarian orientalist Arminius Vámbéry. He lived in New York City from 1938, teaching at the New School for Social Research and was the Hungarian ambassador to the United States from 1947 to 1948. He wrote the introduction to the Hungarian translation of Dr John E. Esslemont's seminal introductory text to the Baháʼí Faith, *Baháʼuʼlláh and the New Era*.

Sir Francis Younghusband (1863–1942) was a British Army officer, explorer, President of the Royal Geographical Society, and writer on foreign policy. Younghusband travelled in the Far East and Central Asia. Around 1904, he had a mystical experience which suffused him with 'love for the whole world' and convinced him that 'men at heart are divine'. He was the founder of the World Congress of Faiths and published a number of books on spiritual themes.

BIBLIOGRAPHY

'Abdu'l-Bahá. *Foundations of World Unity*. Wilmette, Ill.: Bahá'í Publishing Trust, 1972.

— *The Promulgation of Universal Peace*. Wilmette, Ill.: Bahá'í Publishing Trust, 1982.

— *Some Answered Questions*. Haifa: Bahá'í World Centre, 2014.

Bahá'í Prayers. Wilmette, Ill.: Bahá'í Publishing Trust, 1983.

Bahá'í World, The. Vol. II (1926–1928). New York: Bahá'í Publishing Committee, 1928; vol. V (1932–1934). New York: Bahá'í Publishing Committee, 1936; vol. VIII (1938–1940). Wilmette, Ill.: Bahá'í Publishing Committee, 1942; vol. XIII, 1954–1963. Haifa: The Universal House of Justice, 1971. New series: 1994–95. Haifa: Bahá'í World Centre, 1996.

Bahá'u'lláh. *Days of Remembrance*. Haifa: Bahá'í World Centre, 2016.

— *Gems of Divine Mysteries*. Haifa: Bahá'í World Centre, 2002.

— *Gleanings from the Writings of Bahá'u'lláh*. London: Bahá'í Publishing Trust, 1978.

— *The Kitáb-i-Íqán*. Bahá'í Publishing Trust, Wilmette, 1983.

— *Prayers and Meditations by Bahá'u'lláh*. London: Bahá'í Publishing Trust, 1978.

— *The Summons of the Lord of Hosts*. Haifa: Bahá'í World Centre, 2002.

Balyuzi, H. M. *Bahá'u'lláh: A Brief Life*. London: George Ronald, 1972.

Blomfield, Lady. *The Chosen Highway*. London: Bahá'í Publishing Trust, 1940. RP Oxford: George Ronald, 2007.

Cheyne, Thomas Kelly. *The Reconciliation of Races and Religions*. London: Adam and Charles Black, 1914.

Curzon, George N. *Persia and the Persian Question*, Vol. 1. London: Longmans, Green & Co., 1892.

Fathe'azam, Hushmand. *The New Garden*. New Delhi: Bahá'í Publishing Trust, 1958.

Ferraby, John. *All Things Made New*. London: George Allen & Unwin, 1957.

Ford, Mary Hanford. *The Oriental Rose*. New York: Broadway Publishing Company, 1910.

Hayden, Robert. *Collected Poems*. Ed. Frederick Glaysher. New York: Liveright Publishing Corporation, 1985.

Holley, Horace. *Religion for Mankind*. London: George Ronald, 1956.

McNamara, Brendan. *Connections*. Cork: Tusker Keyes, 2007.

Momen, Moojan (ed.). *The Bábí and Bahá'í Religions, 1844–1944: Some Contemporary Western Accounts*. Oxford: George Ronald, 1981.
— *Selections from the Writings of E.G. Browne*. Oxford: George Ronald, 1987.

Nabíl-i-A'ẓam (Muḥammad-i-Zarandí), trans. Shoghi Effendi. *The Dawn-Breakers*. New York: Bahá'í Publishing Committee, 1932.

Shoghi Effendi. *Citadel of Faith: Messages to America 1947–1957*. Wilmette, Ill.: Bahá'í Publishing Trust, 1980.
— *God Passes By*. Wilmette, Ill.: Bahá'í Publishing Trust, 1979.
— *The World Order of Bahá'u'lláh: Selected Letters*. Wilmette, Ill.: Bahá'í Publishing Trust, 1982.

Stendardo, Luigi. *Leo Tolstoy and the Bahá'í Faith*. Oxford: George Ronald Publisher, 1985.

Townshend, George. *Christ and Bahá'u'lláh*. London: George Ronald Publisher, 1985.
— *The Mission of Bahá'u'lláh*. Wilmette, Ill.: Bahá'í Publishing Committee, 1944.
— *The Promise of All Ages*. Oxford: George Ronald Publisher, 1972.

Younghusband, Francis. *The Gleam*. London, John Murray, 1923.

NOTES AND REFERENCES

1. Balyuzí, *Bahá'u'lláh*, p. 9.
2. Shoghi Effendi, *God Passes By*, p. 3.
3. The Universal House of Justice, Riḍván 2018.
4. The Universal House of Justice, To the participants in the forthcoming 114 youth conferences throughout the world, 1 July 2013.
5. The Universal House of Justice, To the Bahá'ís of the World, 21 March 2009.
6. ibid.
7. See Stendardo, *Leo Tolstoy and the Bahá'í Faith*, p. 33.
8. Bahá'u'lláh, *Gleanings from the Writings of Bahá'u'lláh*, XXX.
9. Bahá'u'lláh, Tablet of the Immortal Youth, *Days of Remembrance*, no. 27, par. 3.
10. Bahá'u'lláh, *Gleanings from the Writings of Bahá'u'lláh*, XXXI.
11. Bahá'u'lláh, The Tablet of Aḥmad, *Bahá'í Prayers*.
12. Bahá'u'lláh, *Prayers and Meditations*, LVI.
13. Bahá'u'lláh, *Gems of Divine Mysteries*, par. 91.
14. Bahá'u'lláh, *Gleanings from the Writings of Bahá'u'lláh*, LXXVI.
15. Extracts from Bahá'u'lláh, *Kitáb-i-Íqán*, pp. 230–36.
16. Bahá'u'lláh, Súriy-i-Haykal, *The Summons of the Lord of Hosts*, par. 96.
17. Bahá'u'lláh, *Gleanings from the Writings of Bahá'u'lláh*, CXXXV.
18. Bahá'u'lláh, *Prayers and Meditations,* CLXXVIII.
19. Bahá'u'lláh, excerpt from the Súriy-i-Nush (Súrih of Counsel), in *Days of Remembrance*, no. 35, par. 7–8.
20. 'Abdu'l-Bahá, Talk at Hotel Sacramento, Sacramento, California, 25 October 1912, in *The Promulgation of Universal Peace*, p. 371.
21. 'Abdu'l-Bahá, *Some Answered Questions*, Chapter 8, 'The Báb'.
22. 'Abdu'l-Bahá, Talk at home of Mr. and Mrs. Francis W. Breed, 367 Harvard Street, Cambridge, Massachusetts, 23 May 1912, in *The Promulgation of Universal Peace,* pp. 138–9.
23. 'Abdu'l-Bahá, *Some Answered Questions*, Chapter 9, 'Bahá'u'lláh'.

24. 'Abdu'l-Bahá, Talk at Green Acre, Eliot, Maine, 16 August 1912, in *The Promulgation of Universal Peace*, p. 257.

25. 'Abdu'l-Bahá, 'The Evolution of the Spirit', Talk at 15 Rue Greuze, Paris, 10 November 1911, in *Paris Talks*, no. 29.

26. Shoghi Effendi, *God Passes By*, Chapter 1, pp. 3–5.

27. ibid. Chapter 4, pp. 54–60.

28. Shoghi Effendi, 'The Dispensation of Bahá'u'lláh', in *The World Order of Bahá'u'lláh*, pp. 123–8.

29. Shoghi Effendi, 'The Golden Age of the Cause of Bahá'u'lláh', in *The World Order of Bahá'u'lláh*, pp. 61–2.

30. Shoghi Effendi, 'Centenary of the Martyrdom of the Báb', 4 July 1950, in *Citadel of Faith*, pp. 80–83.

31. Balyuzi, *Bahá'u'lláh*, p. 11.

32. Nabíl-i-A'zam, *The Dawn-Breakers*, Chapter 3, pp. 52–65.

33. ibid. Chapter 2, pp. 25–30.

34. Holley, 'The Revelation of Bahá'u'lláh', in *Religion for Mankind*, pp. 65–6.

35. Holley, 'Papers read at the Conference of Some Living Religions Within the British Empire 1924', in *The Bahá'í World*, vol. II (1926–1928), pp. 228–9.

36. Townshend, *Christ and Bahá'u'lláh*, pp. 64–5.

37. Townshend, 'The Gate of the Dawn', in *The Promise of All Ages*, pp. 88–91.

38. Townshend, Introduction to *The Dawn-Breakers*, pp. xxiii–xxxiii.

39. Townshend, 'Nabíl's History of the Báb', in *The Mission of Bahá'u'lláh*, pp. 19–44.

40. Ferraby, *All Things Made New*, pp. 22–3.

41. Blomfield, *The Chosen Highway*, pp. 29–30.

42. Fathe'azam, *The New Garden*, pp. 29–30.

43. Hanford Ford, *The Oriental Rose*, p. 57.

44. Nicolas, cited in 'References to the Bahá'í Faith', *The Bahá'í World* vol. VIII, p. 625, cited in Momen, *The Bábí and Bahá'í Religions, 1844–1944: Some Contemporary Western Accounts*, p. 38.

45. Hayden, *Collected Poems*, p. 8.

46. Dr William Cormick, cited in McNamara, *Connections*, pp. 12–13.

47. Browne, 'The Bábís of Persia – Their Literature and Doctrines', in *Journal of Royal Asiatic Society, 1889*, p. 933, cited in Momen, *Selections from the Writings of E. G. Browne*, p. 239.

48. Browne, Introduction to Phelps, 'Abbas Effendi, cited in *The Bahá'í World*, vol. XIII, p. 807.

49. Browne, 'Bábíism', cited in Momen, *Selections from the Writings of E.G. Browne*, pp. 426–7.

50. Cheyne, *The Reconciliation of Races and Religions*, p. 74.

51. Vámbéry, 'An Appreciation', cited in *The Bahá'í World*, vol. V, p. 609.
52. See Stendardo, *Leo Tolstoy and the Bahá'í Faith*.
53. Curzon, *Persia and the Persian Question*, vol. 1, pp. 501–2.
54. Younghusband, *The Gleam*, pp. 183–214.
55. Renan, *The Apostles* (1866), cited in *The Bahá'í World*, vol. XIII, pp. 820–21. Translated from the original French (New York: Carleton, 1866), pp. 299–300. Available at https://www.gutenberg.org/files/45081/45081-h/45081-h.htm.
56. Carpenter, *Comparative Religions*, cited in *The Bahá'í World*, vol. XIII, p. 808.